Walking
With Jesus

TIMOTHY CROSS

AMBASSADOR

Walking With Jesus - Milestones in the Life of Christ

© 1995 Timothy Cross

ISBN 1 898787 38 7

Published by
AMBASSADOR PRODUCTIONS LTD.,
16 Hillview Avenue, Belfast, BT5 6JR
Northern Ireland

5333 Commercial Way. Suite 104
Spring Hill, Florida 34606

DEDICATION

To my parents - John and Margaret Cross - with affection, appreciation and admiration.

Contents

Preface

An examination of the life of Jesus Christ can only lead us to exclaim that *God has visited His people* (Luke 7:16). In Jesus Christ, none less than Almighty God Himself became a man and walked upon this planet earth. The life of Christ therefore demands our attention like nothing or no one else. The whole of Christ's earthly life was absolutely incomparable, and yet when we read the Gospels, certain milestones seem to be more prominent than others. The following work will focus on some of these prominent milestones.

Laying my cards on the table at the outset, I admit that this is no cool, clinical study, but written by one possessing a saving interest in Christ, having been enabled by grace to trust Him as my own personal Saviour many years ago. It is also written from the perspective of one who believes that the Bible is the inspired, inerrant Word of God, thus abidingly and crucially relevant for all time. I also confess that in recent months, trials have been such that many earthly hopes have been dashed and cherished dreams taken away. Being a Christian certainly does not mean exemption from life's pain and perplexity. Yet through them all the companionship of Christ remains, giving a blessed silver lining to the clouds. It is my hope and prayer that through a prayerful reading of the following pages, your appreciation of Christ will be the greater, your fellowship with Him the closer, and your devotion

to Him the deeper. May the blessing of the Christ described here
be on you as you read, enabling you to 'love and praise Him more,
His beauties trace, His majesty adore, live near His heart, upon
His bosom lean, obey His voice and all His will esteem.'

Timothy J. E. Cross
Porthcawl
South Wales

CHAPTER ONE

The Milestone Of His Birth

> Be not afraid; for behold, I bring you good news of a great joy
> which will come to all the people; for to you is born this day in
> the city of David a Saviour, who is Christ the Lord
> (Luke 2:10,11).

The birth of any baby is always a special milestone. Christ's birth at Bethlehem two thousand years ago though was so momentous that it split time into BC and AD.

At Bethlehem, none less than God became man and was born, for *the Word became flesh and dwelt among us* (John 1:14). At Bethlehem the infinite became an infant; at Bethlehem the uncreated Creator entered into His creation; at Bethlehem the eternal entered into time, for there, the Son of God became a Son of man, that the children of men might become the children of God. What a milestone this was, filling the very heavens with praise (Luke 2:13 ff). The Event was and always will be incomparable. One of the earliest Christian hymns celebrated it in song thus: *Great indeed, we confess is the mystery of our religion: God was manifested in the flesh* (1 Timothy 3:16).

At Christmas-time, we in the British Commonwealth gather around our TV's and radios to listen to a message from our Queen. At the first Christmas though, Luke records for us a message sent straight from heaven. The message went as follows: *to you is born this day in the city of David a Saviour who is Christ the Lord*

(Luke 2:11). These words deserve our attention and scrutiny more so than the words of any earthly monarch, for they are of eternal moment. They inform us about the nativity of God:- 1. The Place of the Nativity, 2. The Person of the Nativity, 3. The Purpose of the Nativity, and 4. The Pertinence of the Nativity.

1. The Place of the Nativity

born this day in the city of David . . .

Jesus was born in Bethlehem, the city of David. David was Israel's greatest earthly king. Jesus, being in the same genealogy and earthly line of king David, has been referred to by the Church justly as 'great David's Greater Son', for He is the *King of kings and Lord of lords* (Revelation 19:16). It was no accident that Jesus was born at Bethlehem, even though it seemed more likely that He would be born at Nazareth, the home of His earthly parents. He was destined to be born at Bethlehem because God had ordained it so, speaking through His prophet Micah four hundred years previously *But you, O Bethlehem Ephrathah, who are little to be among the clans of Judah, from you shall come forth for me one who is to be ruler in Israel, whose origin is from of old, from ancient days* (Micah 5:2).

The birth of Christ is history not mythology, fact not fiction. The 'little town of Bethlehem' can be pointed out quite precisely on a world map. The first Christmas actually occurred in time and space. Writing from here on the South Wales coast, I could take a bus to Heathrow, London. From there I could take a plane to Tel Aviv, Israel. From Tel Aviv I could get a bus to Jerusalem, then from Jerusalem I could catch another bus which would take me to a town five miles south-west – the town of Bethlehem.

Bethlehem Ephrathah. Bethlehem' means 'house of bread.' This is so because it is surrounded by grain fields (see the book of Ruth). How fitting for Jesus to be born here, as He once said of Himself *I am the bread of life. He who comes to me shall not hunger and he who believes in me shall never thirst* (John 5:35). 'Ephrathah,' the district, means 'fruitful.' Again, how fitting for Jesus to be born in such a district, for He said *I am the true vine . . . He who abides in me and I in him, he it is that bears much fruit, for apart from me you can do nothing* (John 15:1,5). 'Bread': 'Fruitful'. With a little thought we can see the emblems of Calvary here at the place of Christ's birth. The Church commemorates Christ's death at Calvary as He commanded, in the eating of bread and the drinking of wine. Bread is the product of crushed grain. Wine is the product of crushed grapes. Salvation is the product of Calvary. Christ went through the mill and heat of Calvary to save our souls. At Calvary Christ shed His *blood of the new covenant . . . poured out for many for the forgiveness of sins* (Matthew 26:28).

Interestingly, the first ever mention of Bethlehem in the Bible is in Genesis 35:19. It is associated here with Jacob's wife Rachel giving birth to Benjamin. In giving birth to Benjamin, Rachel died. With her last gasp, she gave him the name 'Benoni' which means 'son of my sorrow' – but she was over-ruled by her husband Jacob who named the child 'Benjamin' meaning 'son of my right hand' (see Genesis 35:18). Significantly, when Jesus was born at Bethlehem almost two thousand years later, He fulfilled both names in His one person. 'Son of my sorrow' : 'Son of my right hand'. Jesus was *a man of sorrows, and acquainted with grief* (Isaiah 53:3). Jesus is the one *who is at the right hand of God* (Romans 8:34 et al). The place of the nativity then was and is most significant in bibilical history.

2. The Person of the Nativity

to you is born . . . Christ the Lord

i. His Birth

Whilst the birth of Christ was normal, His conception most definitely was not. Significantly, it is *Luke the beloved physician* (Colossians 4:14) who devotes more space to 'the Virgin Birth of Christ' than any other Gospel writer. Who better than a medical doctor, well trained in gynaecology, to relate such matters? Whilst Matthew records tersely that Mary *was found to be with child of the Holy Spirit* (Matthew 1:18), Luke, as it were, takes us into the surgery, allowing us to listen to the angel explaining to Mary how *The Holy Spirit will come upon you, and the power of the Most High will overshadow you; therefore the child to be born will be called holy, the Son of God* (Luke 1:35). We have seen how the place of Christ's birth was prophecied by Micah four hundred years previously. Likewise, the manner of Christ's birth had also been prophecied by Micah's contemporary Isaiah. In Isaiah 7:14 we read the prophecy *Behold, a virgin shall conceive and bear a son, and shall call His name Immanuel.* Matthew, the most Jewish of the Gospels takes pains to point out that Christ's birth of a virgin *took place to fulfil what the Lord had spoken by the prophet: 'Behold, a virgin shall conceive and bear a son, and His name shall be called Emmanuel' (which means, God with us)* (Matthew 1:22,23).

The virgin birth of Christ is a Christian fundamental. The so called 'Apostle's Creed', an early, minimal statement of the Christian Faith states He was 'born of the virgin Mary.' The miraculous, virgin birth of Christ comes in for its periodic mocking, even by so called 'Christian leaders'. The true believer though knows that *with God nothing will be impossible* (Luke 1:37), as miracles present no difficulty to omnipotence. The virgin birth of Christ was essential, for had He been conceived in the normal way of Adam's descendents, He would have inherited Adam's sin. The virgin birth is essential because it takes a sinless one to redeem sinners – and such a sinless one was the One born at Bethlehem.

ii. His Being

Christ the Lord.

The One born at Bethlehem was no ordinary person. Christ is His title. It means 'the anointed one' – revealing Jesus as the longed for Messiah and fulfilment of all the Old Testament hopes.

How the Jews longed for the expected and prophecied Agent of God who would come in and inaugurate the Kingdom of Heaven. In Jesus He arrived! Peter was to confess to Jesus some thirty years later *You are the Christ, the Son of the living God* (Matthew 16:16). Luke records of godly old Simeon that *it had been revealed to Him by the Spirit that he should not see death before he had seen the Lord's Christ* (Luke 2:26). On seeing the infant Christ, with great joy, Simeon *took Him up in his arms and blessed God and said, 'Lord, now lettest thou Thy servant depart in peace, according to Thy word, for mine eyes have seen Thy salvation . . .* (Luke 2:28-30).

Notice though that the One born is described as Christ *the Lord*. The title 'Lord' is a title of deity - a title of God Himself. *I am the LORD, and there is no other, besides me there is no God* (Isaiah 45:5). This being so, we may state that Christianity is Christ, and Christ is God! *Emmanuel, (which means God with us) (Matthew 1:23).* Doubting Thomas was not rebuked for idolatry when He bowed before Jesus and exclaimed *My Lord and my God* (John 20:28). *Jesus is Lord* (1 Corinthians 12:3) is agreed as being the earliest credal statement of the Christian Faith:-

Christ by highest heaven adored
Christ the everlasting Lord
Late in time behold Him come
Offspring of a virgin's womb
Veiled in flesh the Godhead see
Hail the incarnate Deity
Pleased as Man with men to dwell
Jesus our Immanuel

3. The Purpose of the Nativity

To you is born . . . A SAVIOUR . . .

The Christian Gospel is the good news of a Saviour. The word 'Saviour' means a rescuer, or a deliverer. Salvation is a result of being saved by the Saviour. The Bible is crystal clear in that the one overriding and overarching purpose of the birth of Christ was the sinner's salvation: *You shall call His name Jesus for He will SAVE His people from their sins* (Matthew 1:21). *The saying is sure and worthy of full acceptance, that Christ Jesus came into the world to SAVE sinners* (1 Timothy 1:15).

In being born to be our Saviour, we face the paradox that Jesus was born, not so much to live, but to die. The cross overshadows the cradle, for His incarnation was with a view to His immolation. The Bible says that *without the shedding of blood there is no forgiveness of sins* (Hebrews 9:22), and it was on the cross, thirty three years later, that Jesus died, shedding His *blood of the new covenant, . . .poured out for many for the forgiveness of sins* (Matthew 26:28), so that whoever believes in Him may be assured of pardon for sin and peace with God.

The Gospel then is good news. In being the good news of a divine Saviour however, it implies the background of the bad news of human sin. The bad news is that we need to be saved, and we need to be saved because we are, by nature, sinners, and as sinners, under God's righteous condemnation. *If we say we have no sin we deceive ourselves and the truth is not in us* (1 John 1:8). *None is righteous, no, not one . . . all have sinned and fall short of the glory of God* (Romans 3:10, 23). We certainly need to be saved, and in the Saviour, we have the anwer to our need. Trusting in the One born at Bethlehem for salvation, and in Him alone, is a crucial matter, for *there is salvation in no one else, for there is no other name under heaven, given among men, by which we must be saved* (Acts 4:12). This brings us finally to:-

4. The Pertinence of the Nativity

TO YOU is born this day in the city of David a Saviour, who is Christ the Lord . . .

Jesus came to save real people. The people addressed in our verse were lowly shepherds, despised by men but loved by God. It is often the case that the candidates for salvation are rather unlikely. Paul writing to some Christians at Corinth said *For consider your call, brethren; not many of you were wise according to worldly standards, not many were powerful, not many were of noble birth; but God chose what is foolish in the world to shame the wise, God chose what is weak in the world to shame the strong, God chose what is low and despised in the world, even things that are not, to bring to nothing things that are, so that no human being might boast in the presence of God* (1 Corinthians 1:26-29).

An unpopular truth, even in the 'evangelical' world, is that Jesus did not come into the world to save everyone. He came only to save God's elect. In John 17:2 we read Jesus talking to His Father about these: *Thou hast given Him power over all flesh, to give eternal life to all whom Thou hast given Him.* Christ then, came into the world to save God's elect, and if we are aware of our sin and have heard the Gospel call, and have been enabled by divine grace to cast ourselves solely upon Christ for full salvation, we may be sure that we are one of God's elect, for *those whom He predestined He also called* (Romans 8:30). Those whom God has chosen for salvation in Christ will most certainly be made willing and able to come to Christ. Jesus said *All that the Father gives to me will come to me; and him who comes to me I will not cast out* (John 6:37).

Bethlehem then was not the beginning of the eternal Son of God. Far from it. *In the beginning was the Word, and the Word was with God, and the Word was God* (John 1:1). Yet Bethlehem's soil marks the hallowed first milestone in the earthly life of Christ. Bethlehem marks the dawning of redemption, for there God's Son was born, that we might be born again.

See! in yonder manger low
Born for us on earth below
See! the Lamb of God appears
Promised from eternal years

Hail, thou ever-blessed morn!
Hail, redemption's happy dawn!
Sing through all Jerusalem
Christ is born in Bethlehem

CHAPTER TWO

The Milestone Of His Baptism

Then Jesus came from Galilee to the Jordan to John, to be baptized by
him. John would have prevented Him, saying, 'I need to be baptized
by you, and do you come to me?' But Jesus answered him, 'Let it be
so now; for thus it is fitting for us to fulfil all righteousness.' Then he
consented. And when Jesus was baptized, He went up immediately
from the water, and behold, the heavens were opened and He saw the
Spirit of God descending like a dove, and alighting on Him; and lo, a
voice from heaven, saying, 'This is my beloved Son, with whom I am
well pleased' (Matthew 3:13-17).

If you have ever attended a Christian baptismal service, you
will know just what special and significant occasions they are.
Baptism - whether adult or infant - marks a important milestone in a person's life, and is looked back upon and dated until
one's dying day.

The Lord Jesus Christ was also baptised. His baptism was a
special milestone in His life too, as in many ways it marked the
commencement of His earthly ministry proper. It is obviously an
important milestone in the life of Christ, because the Holy Spirit
has seen fit to record it for posterity no less than three times in
Holy Scripture – see Matthew 3:13-17; Mark 1:9-11 and Luke
3:21-22. This being so, let us consider this important milestone of
the baptism of the King of kings from four viewpoints:- 1. The
Setting, 2. The Sign, 3. The Spirit, and 4. The Sound.

1. The Setting

Jesus came from Galilee to the JORDAN to John , to be baptised . . .

Whilst the crowds may have been unaware of what was going on, they were actually standing at a turning point in the world's history. Jesus left His trade at the carpenter's bench and began His three years of public ministry – a ministry which would lead Him eventually to die on a cruel cross to save His people from their sins. His ministry commenced though with His going through the waters of baptism in the River Jordan.

The name 'Jordan' means 'descender'. The Jordan is the main river in Israel, flowing from the north of Israel down to the Dead Sea in the south. It is mentioned many times in the Old Testament, and even today is essential as regards Israel's water supply.

Jesus' baptism in the Jordan has an interesting parallel in the life of His name sake Joshua, over one and a half thousand years before this time. Joshua, Moses' successor, also began his ministry at the river Jordan. The Israelites even celebrated it in song: *The sea looked and fled, Jordan turned back . . . What ails you, O sea that you flee? O Jordan, that you turn back?* (Psalm 114:3,5). Joshua then commenced at the Jordan and went on to the military conquest of Canaan. Jesus likewise commenced at the Jordan, but He went on to the spiritual conquest at Calvary. As has already been intimated, the name 'Jesus' is the Greek form of the Hebrew 'Joshua' or 'Yeshua.' Both mean 'God is salvation.' We may state confidently of Jesus though 'Behold, a greater than Joshua is here,' for Jesus actually appeared to Joshua in one of the Old Testament 'theophanies' or pre-incarnate appearances, and was worshipped by him. Joshua 5:13 ff relates the happening. *Joshua . . . looked and behold, a man stood before him with His drawn sword in His hand; and Joshua went to Him and said to Him, 'Are you for us or for our adversaries?' And He said, 'No, but as commander of the army of the Lord I have now come.'*

*And Joshua fell on His face to the earth, and worshipped Him . . .
And the commander of the Lord's army said to Joshua, 'Put off
your shoes from your feet; for the place where you stand is holy.'
And Joshua did so.* Jesus then is the One worshipped by Joshua.
He is the commander of the Lord's army, and captain of our salva-
tion.

Continuing the parallel, we recall that the book of Joshua began
at the River Jordan, and under Joshua's leadership the land of
Canaan - the promised land, flowing with milk and honey - was
conquered and colonised, coming into the possession of Israel.
Towards the end of this book which began at the Jordan we read
*Not one of all the good promises which the Lord made to the house
of Israel failed; all came to pass* (Joshua 21:45).

There is a spiritual parallel to this in the life of Jesus. His ministry too began at the Jordan, but because of His conquest, whoever believes in Him is assured of a home which makes Canaan
seem inferior by comparison for *What no eye has seen, nor ear
heard, nor the heart of man conceived what God has prepared for
those who love Him* (1 Corinthians 2:9). Just as God fulfilled all
His promises to ancient Israel through Joshua, so God does and
will fulfil all His promises to His Israel the Church through Jesus.
Not one of His promises will fail, but all will come to pass for *the
Son of God, Jesus Christ, . . . was not Yes and No; but in Him it is
always Yes, for all the promises of God find their Yes in Him* (2
Corinthians 1:19,20). In Jesus we have the *hope of eternal life
which God, who never lies, promised ages ago, and at the proper
time manifested in His word through the preaching . . .* (Titus
1:2,3).

2. The Sign

Jesus was baptised

It is no wonder that John had hesitations about baptising Jesus.
Luke 3:3 explains his baptism as *a baptism of repentance for the
forgiveness of sins.* In being the sinless Son of God, with Whom

God was well pleased, Jesus had no requirement to repent, and no need of forgiveness. *He knew no sin* said Paul (2 Corinthians 5:21), *in Him there is no sin* said John (1 John 3:5), *He committed no sin,* said Peter (1 Peter 2:22). Yet Jesus insisted that John baptise Him *Let it be so now; for thus it is fitting for us to fulfil all righteousness* (v.15). We see here then Jesus, the sinless One, identifying Himself with the sinful humanity He came to save. He came down to our level to raise us up to His. He fulfilled all righteousness. He took upon Himself the yoke of the law to redeem us who have broken God's law. He was obedient unto death, and His obedience avails for Adam's disobedient race.

Jesus's baptism in water pictures and prefigures His work of redemption. In Baptism water passes over the one baptised. When the sign was applied to Jesus it pointed beyond itself to His real Baptism – His baptism of death. In Luke 12:50 He stated *I have a baptism to be baptised with; and how I am constrained until it is accomplished.* He also asked James and John when they sought glory without suffering *Are you able to drink the cup that I drink, or to be baptised with the baptism with which I am baptised?* (Mark 10:38).

The ultimate baptism in Jesus's life was His baptism of death on Calvary's tree. There He went through the awesome baptism of bearing our sins and God's holy wrath and righteous judgment upon them so we might be saved. Water baptism can involve being submerged in water momentarily, the water passing over one's head. Calvary was prophecied using similar imagery: *Thy wrath lies heavy upon me, and Thou dost overwhelm me with all Thy waves* (Psalm 88:7), *All Thy waves and Thy billows have gone over me* (Psalm 42:7). Then Jonah - a clear Old Testament type of the Lord Jesus - wrote of his own experience: *Thou didst cast me into the deep, into the heart of the seas, and the flood was round about me. All Thy waves and Thy billows passed over me* (Jonah 2:3).

On the Cross therefore Jesus received His real baptism. It was there that He bore the full brunt of God's holy wrath on our sins, being judged so that we might be justified and assured that *There is therefore now no condemnation for those who are in Christ Jesus* (Romans 8:1).

3. The Spirit

Although Jesus had actually been conceived by the Holy Spirit (see Luke 1:35), when He commenced His ministry He would have needed a special endowment of the Holy Spirit's power. This He received at His baptism when *behold, the heavens were opened and he saw the Spirit of God descending like a dove, and alighting on Him.*

In the Old Testament, prophets, priests and kings were all anointed with oil as they commenced their office, ministry and service. Oil was a symbol of the Holy Spirit. Being anointed with oil symbolised being set apart, consecrated and equipped to serve God and His people. Jesus then also received a special unction from the Spirit of God as He began His ministry.

Jesus's special anointing by the Holy Spirit at His baptism is a graphic reminder that He is the Messiah. The Greek for 'Messiah' is 'Christ', meaning 'the anointed one.' The Old Testament without the New could be considered as one long Messianic longing - a longing for the promised Redeemer and Agent of God Who would come to earth and bring in the Kingdom of Heaven. The New Testament leaves us in no doubt that Jesus fulfilled all these Old Testament hopes and desires. He is the Messiah - the anointed one. Peter told how *God anointed Jesus of Nazareth with the Holy Spirit and with power* (Acts 10:38), and Jesus said of His own mission *The Spirit of the Lord is upon me, because He has anointed me to preach good news to the poor* (Luke 4:18).

We have already alluded to the fact that in the Old Testament, prophets, priests and kings were all anointed with oil as they began their ministries. As Christ, Jesus exercises all three offices of prophet, priest and king in His one Person. The *Shorter Catechism* puts it best when it defines:-

'Christ executeth the office of a prophet in revealing to us
by His Word and Spirit the will of God for our salvation.
'Christ executeth the office of a priest in His once offering
up of Himself a sacrifice to satisfy divine justice and rec-
oncile us to God, and in making continual intercession for
us.
'Christ executeth the office of a king in subduing us to
Himself, in ruling and defending us and in restraining and
conquering all His and our enemies.'

As an interesting aside, notice that at Jesus's baptism the Bible
describes the Holy Spirit descending upon Him *like a dove*. The
dove is a lovely image of God's purity and peace. But did you
know that the name 'Jonah' means 'dove'? The prophet Jonah, as
we have seen, also received a 'baptism' and we have it on the
authority of Jesus that Jonah was a type of Himself: *For as Jonah
was three days and three nights in the belly of the whale, so will
the Son of Man be three days and three nights in the heart of the
earth* (Matthew 12:40). Finally though, what of:-

4. The Sound

*Lo, a voice from heaven, saying 'This is my beloved Son,
with whom I am well pleased.'*

What a testimony! Jesus had been through the rough and tum-
ble of childhood, the perils of adolescense, and the give, take and
graft of work and early manhood, and God's verdict on it all was
'well pleased.'

Three times in the Gospels a voice from heaven is heard bearing witness to Jesus - here, again at His Transfiguration and again
in John 12:28 during the last week of His ministry. Man's opinion
of Jesus varied and still varies. "Who do men say that I am?" Jesus asked once. Many religious and irreligious answers have been
proffered throughout the centuries, but surely this Voice from above
at His baptism ends all arguments as regards Christ's identity. God
says of Him *THIS IS MY BELOVED SON*. Jesus is the Son of
God and God the Son.

The Voice from on high reveals to us two things:-

i. Christ as Son - His Special Relationship
ii. Christ as Servant - His Saving Redemption

i. Christ as Son: His Special Relationship

Jesus is the eternal Son of God. His sonship is unique. By nature we are the children of wrath, but by nature He is the Son of God, the second Person of the Trinity. Our sonship - if we are Christians - is based on His. We are adopted as sons through *the* Son. Christ's relationship to His Father then is a *distinctive* relationship, for God has only one only begotten Son. But also, Christ's relationship to His Father is a *dear* relationship – He is His *beloved Son* with Whom He had a holy infatuation.

ii. Christ as Servant: His Saving Redemption

The Voice from heaven at Jesus's baptism seems to have two distinct Old Testament echoes. In Psalm 2:7 God says *You are my Son, today I have begotten you*, and in Isaiah 42:1, glimpsing Jesus as the Servant of God, we read God's saying of Him: *Behold my servant, whom I uphold, my chosen in whom my soul delights; I have put my Spirit upon Him, He will bring forth justice to the nations.* The Son of God then is also the Servant of God, and from the mouth of Jesus Himself we know that His servanthood is inseparable from His sacrifice as *The Son of Man also came not to be served but to serve, and to give His life as a ransom for many* (Mark 10:45).

And so, as we go back to the milestone of Jesus's baptism, we already see the cross overshadowing His life. His baptism looked forward to Calvary - redemption anticipated - just as today baptism looks back to Calvary, where redemption was accomplished - accomplished for time and eternity, when Christ sealed His ministry commenced here with the triumphant cry *It is finished* (John 19:30).

On Jordan's bank He stands
Impressive, lovely sight
Obedient to the Law's demands
The Father's chief delight!

The Father loves the Son
Who ever pleased Him well
Each movement of that Holy One
Some beauty forth doth tell

CHAPTER THREE

The Milestone Of His Temptation

Then Jesus was led up by the Spirit into the wilderness to be tempted by the devil. And He fasted forty days and forty nights, and afterward He was hungry. And the tempter came and said to Him, 'If you are the Son of God, command these stones to become loaves of bread.' But He answered, 'It is written, 'Man shall not live by bread alone, but by every word that proceeds from the mouth of God.'' Then the devil took Him to the holy city, and set Him on the pinnacle of the temple, and said to Him, 'If you are the Son of God, throw yourself down; for it is written, 'He will give His angels charge of you,' and 'On their hands they will bear you up, lest you strike your foot against a stone.'' Jesus said to him, 'Again it is written, 'You shall not tempt the Lord your God.'' Again, the devil took Him to a very high mountain, and showed Him all the kingdoms of the world and the glory of them; and he said to Him, 'All these I will give you, if you will fall down and worship me.' Then Jesus said to him, 'Begone Satan! for it is written, 'You shall worship the Lord your God and Him only shall you serve.'' Then the devil left Him, and behold, angels came and ministered to Him (Matthew 4:1-11).

Have you ever noticed in your life that times of blessing are often followed by times of buffetting? A blessed Sunday, for example, often precedes some testing trouble, trial or calamity the following week. It is as though God prepares us for what is ahead by giving us special grace in advance.

It may surprise you to know that this pattern of a hard time following on from a good time can be seen in the life of Jesus, and this is especially so here in His temptations in the Judean wilderness. No sooner had God said *'This is my beloved Son'* (Matthew 3:17) than *Then Jesus was led up by the Spirit into the wilderness to be tempted by the devil* (Matthew 4:1). (The original Scriptures did not have our chapter divisions). The devil then proceeded to test the very Sonship that heaven had declared by seeking to sow the doubt *'If you are the Son of God . . .'* (Matthew 4:3,6).

The Holy Spirit has ensured that the temptation of Jesus in the wilderness has been recorded no less than three times in the Bible – see Matthew 4:1-11, Mark 1:12-13 and Luke 4:1-13. It has much to instruct us about both our Saviour and ourselves. As all Scripture points to Christ in some way, it comes as no surprise when we see Christ's experience in the wilderness paralleled and contrasted elsewhere in the Bible. For example, the first Adam was also tempted by Satan, not however in a dry, desolate desert, but in the perfect, most fruitful environment of Paradise. But whereas Jesus triumphed over Satan, Adam succumbed to his enticements. Similarly, whereas Jesus was tested in the wilderness for forty days after His baptism, so likewise with the people of Israel for forty years after they had been *through the sea . . .* and *baptised into Moses* (1 Corinthians 10:1,2). The Lord was to remind these ancient Israelites *you shall remember all the way which the Lord your God has led you these forty years in the wilderness, that He might humble you, testing you to know what was in your heart . . .* (Deuteronomy 8:2). Needless to say again, where Israel proved to be a failure, Jesus was proved victorious.

Let us then look in further detail at this incident the Holy Spirit has given to us three times. I have drawn out six points for our consideration: 1. The Spirit, 2. The Satan ,3. The Scriptures, 4. The Sympathy, 5. The Sinlessness, 6. The Saviour.

1. The Spirit

Then Jesus was led up by the Spirit into the wilderness to be tempted . . .

The wilderness is an awful, barren, desolate place, characterised by deadness. Everything in the wilderness which is not of God dies – and yet it was God's Spirit Who led Jesus to such a place, as indeed He may lead us into a spiritual wilderness, seeking to deepen our faith, taking away all our man-made props, leaving us totally and utterly dependant upon God alone.

It is comforting to know that this trial of Jesus and all of our trials come ultimately, not from Satan, but from God. There has always been an erroneous 'dualistic' view which sees all good from God and all evil from Satan. The Bible though, on the contrary, assures us *from Him and through Him and to Him are all things . . .* (Romans 11:36). Even Satan's buffettings are under God's control and limitation. God, as it were, controls the thermostat and will never test us beyond what He sees good for us (1 Corinthians 10:13, and the whole book of Job). It is necessary of course to point out James 1:13:- *Let no one say when he is tempted 'I am tempted by God'; for God cannot be tempted with evil and He Himself tempts no one*; and yet mysteriously, whilst God is not the author of evil, His omnipotence is such that He even uses evil to accomplish His greater purposes – the ultimate example of this being the Cross. All this being so, we can be assured that the trials and difficulties in our own personal 'wildernesses' are not by chance, but for our good. *We know that in everything God works for good with those who love Him* (Romans 8:28).

> *Every joy or trial, falleth from above*
> *Hidden on the dial, of the Sun of love*
> *We may trust Him fully, all for us to do*
> *Those who trust Him wholly, find Him wholly true*

2. The Satan

to be tempted by the devil

If we believe that the Bible is the inspired, inerrant Word of God, we have no option but to believe in a personal devil – current fashion and scorn notwithstanding. The *Lion Concise Bible Encyclopaedia* defines the devil as 'the being who personifies all that is evil and opposed to God . . . Satan is the one who tries to tempt people to do wrong so that he can accuse them before God.'

It is a biblical axiom that if we are Christians, we have Christ as our Friend and the devil as our foe. The enemy of Jesus is also the enemy of every Christian. Peter warned *Be sober, be watchful. Your adversary the devil prowls around like a roaring lion, seeking some one to devour* (1 Peter 5:8). Paul exhorts us to *Put on the whole armour of God that you may be able to stand against the wiles of the devil* (Ephesians 6:11). The devil's power should neither be under nor overestimated. He is mighty – but God is almighty. The devil is exceedingly cunning – and yet he is impotent against Omnipotent Omniscience.

Our account here records Satan as tempting and testing Jesus in two areas, as regards i. His Sonship - the Person of Christ ii. His Strategy - the Programme of Christ. In Jesus's weak, starved physical condition, he sought to doubt His unique Sonship and avert and divert Him from the will of God, with its costly obedience, into the by-path meadow of some less costly, easier way. Principal J. Oswald Sanders summarises the devil's three temptations of Jesus thus:-

1. The first was the temptation to satisfy a legitimate appetite by illegitimate means (stones into loaves).
2. The second was the temptation to produces spiritual results by unspiritual means (jumping off the pinnacle of the temple).
3. The third was the temptation to obtain a lawful heritage by unlawful means (worshipping Satan).

But the devil did not succeed. How ever could he? The earliest Gospel promise had prophesied to Satan of Christ *He shall bruise your head* (Genesis 3:15). John informs us *The reason the Son of God appeared was to destroy the works of the devil* (1 John 3:8), and the whole of Jesus's earthly life was one victorious triumph over the devil, a triumph culminating at Calvary whereby *through death He might destroy him who has the power of death, that is the devil, and deliver all those who through fear of death were subject to life long bondage* (Hebrews 2:14,15).

3. The Scriptures

Note well that *the Scriptures* were the means by which Jesus combatted Satan. Jesus responded to the three temptations three times with *It is written* (4:4,6,10). The earthly life of our Lord reveals that He was steeped in the Scriptures – and what was indispensible for the sinless redeemer in His temptations is surely much more indispensible for us redeemed sinners in facing our trials and temptations. Part of the necessary armour which God has provided for us to combat Satan is *the sword of the Spirit, which is the Word of God* (Ephesians 6:17). The Psalmist wrote *I have laid up Thy Word in my heart, that I might not sin against Thee* (Psalm 119:11). The apostle John wrote *I write to you, young men, because you are strong, and the Word of God abides in you, and you have overcome the evil one* (1 John 2:14). This being so, oh to know, obey and apply the Scriptures better! In many ways this is a simple matter of diligent, daily, prayerful study – verse by verse, chapter by chapter, book by book. *Let the Word of Christ dwell in you richly* (Colossians 3:16).

4. The Sympathy

The fact that Christ was no stranger to temptation is a source of great solace to us in our temptations. How good it is to know that Jesus has 'been there before us' and knows from first-hand experience something of the difficulties and distresses we face. In Christ, God, as it were, entered into the thick of the battle. Even though Jesus was the Son of God, He had no special privileges which exempted Him from temptation and suffering. No other religion offers such a Divine Solidarity. *For because He Himself has suffered and been tempted, He is able to help those who are tempted*

(Hebrews 2:18). We cannot and dare not say of our God "He will never really know what it is like" for in the Person of His Son we have One who can *sympathise with our weaknesses . . . one who in every respect has been tempted as we are, yet without sin* (Hebrews 4:15).

> *Touched with a sympathy within*
> *He knows our feeble frame*
> *He knows what sore temptations means,*
> *For He has felt the same.*

5. The Sinlessness

The temptations of Christ, both here and throughout His earthly life, reveal to us His total and immaculate sinlessness - what the theologians call His 'impeccability'. Jesus never once gave in to temptation for He could never. We therefore have to hold two New Testament truths in tension:- i. Christ is like us. ii. Christ is totally unlike us. Hebrews 4:15 again: *one who in every respect has been tempted as we are, yet without sin.*

> *But spotless, innocent, and pure*
> *The great Redeemer stood*
> *While Satan's fiery darts He bore*
> *And did resist to blood.*

Only a sinless One could redeem sinners, for only a sinless One could offer Himself on Calvary's altar as a sacrificial *Lamb without blemish or spot* (1 Peter 1:19).

It is well-nigh impossible for us who have been 'born in sin and shapen in iniquity' to comprehend what it would be like to be sinless – to never think a wrong thought, say a bad word or do a bad deed and suffer a guilty conscience. Yet we are impelled and compelled to say that Christ just could not sin. It is unthinkable that He could, due to His divine nature and constitution and the communication of the properties between His human and divine nature. The three wilderness temptations here reveal His sinlessness most plainly. He was not so much sinless because He triumphed over temptation (though He did), rather, it was *because* He was sinless that He triumphed over temptation. The temptations of Christ revealed what He was like – just as our temptations, on a shameful level, reveal what we are like.

We admittedly are facing a mystery here. It is objected that if Christ could not sin, He could not have felt temptation's pull. It is healthy here to admit our ignorance, and state the seeming paradox that both:- i. Christ could not sin ii. Christ's temptations were real – His forty days without food were no fiction. Perhaps we should expect paradox when we are dealing with the Son of God. How dare we try and fit Him into our puny mental framework. The truth here is at 'both extremes' and far greater than our comprehension of it. Let us hold in tension what the Bible records: *This man receives sinners and eats with them* (Luke 15:2) along with His being *holy, blameless, unstained, separated from sinners* (Hebrews 7:26).

> The wilderness with each
> Deep testing doth but show
> No evil shaft His soul could reach
> No tempter Him o'erthrow.

6. The Saviour

In our introduction we intimated that this incident of our Saviour's temptation in the wilderness reveals Christ as the Second Adam, or more correctly, the Last Adam. He triumphed where Adam failed. He was obedient where Adam was disobedient. Scripture makes much of this contrast and its consequences:- *For as by one man's disobedience many were made sinners, so by one man's obedience many will be made righteous* (Romans 5:19).

Christ's triumph over temptation, along with His sinlessness, brings us to what Reformed theologians call the 'Active Obedi-

ence of Christ' – that is, His total obedience to God and His fulfilment of the Law in the sinner's stead, merits eternal life for all
who are united to Him as their federal head. Back in Eden, God
promised eternal life to the first Adam (and by implication to all
his descendants) on condition of perfect obedience. The *Westminster Confession* states 'The first covenant made with man was a
covenant of works, wherein life was promised to Adam, and in
him to all his posterity, upon condition of perfect and personal
obedience' (VII,II). And we all know what happened – Adam diso-
beyed God and so brought death on all his descendants.

Christ's 'active obedience' however undoes the dire and drastic
consequence of Adam's disobedience. His 'active obedience'
merits for us eternal life! There is a sense in which, if we are
Christ's, we can say that His life was as much in our place as His
death. Louis Berkhof clarifies this point most helpfully:-

> 'Christ as Mediator entered the federal relation in which
> Adam stood in the state of integrity, in order to merit eter-
> nal life for the sinner. This constitutes the active obedi-
> ence of Christ, consisting in all that Christ did to observe
> the law in its federal aspect, as the condition for obtaining
> eternal life. The active obedience of Christ was necessary
> to make His passive obedience (that is His death on the
> Cross for our sins) acceptable with God . . . if Christ had
> not rendered active obedience, the human nature of Christ
> itself would have fallen short of the just demands of God,
> and He would not have been able to atone for others . . .
> 'If Christ had merely obeyed the law and had not also paid
> the penalty, He would not have won a title to eternal life
> for sinners; and if He had merely paid the penalty, without
> meeting the original demands of the law, He would have
> left man in the position of Adam before the fall, still
> comfronted with the task of obtaining eternal life by way
> of obedience. By His active obedience, however, He car-
> ried His people beyond that point and gave them a claim to
> eternal life.' (*Systematic Theology* , pp. 380,381).

Christ then was tempted yet triumphant. He spoke the truth when He said of Satan *He has no power over me; but I do as the Father has commanded me* (John 14:30,31). And the good news is that if we are Christ's we are partakers of His triumph. His triumph over Satan in the wilderness in the early stages of His earthly ministry, was one of the early links of the 'salvation chain' leading to His being *obedient unto death, even death on a cross* (Philippians 2:8), bringing deliverance from bondage to Satan and eternal life for all who trust in Him.

Forty days and forty nights
Thou was tempted in the wild
Forty days and forty nights
Tempted and yet undefiled

And if Satan waxing sore
Flesh or spirit should assail
Thou his vanquisher before
Grant we may not faint nor fail.

CHAPTER FOUR

The Milestone Of His First Miracle

On the third day there was a marriage at Cana in Galilee, and the mother of Jesus was there; Jesus also was invited to the marriage, with His disciples. When the wine gave out, the mother of Jesus said to Him, 'They have no wine.' And Jesus said to her, 'O woman, what have you to do with me? My hour has not yet come.' His mother said to the servants, 'Do whatever He tells you.' Now six stone jars were standing there, for the Jewish rites of purification, each holding twenty or thirty gallons. Jesus said to them, 'Fill the jars with water.' And they filled them up to the brim. He said to them, 'Now draw some out, and take it to the steward of the feast.' So they took it. When the steward of the feast tasted the water now become wine, and did not know where it came from (though the servants who had drawn the water knew), the steward of the feast called the bridegroom and said to him, 'Every man serves the good wine first; and when men have drunk freely, then the poor wine; but you have kept the good wine until now.' This, the first of His signs, Jesus did at Cana in Galilee, and manifested His glory; and His disciples believed in Him (John 2:1-11.)

Firsts make such an indelible impression on our minds that we remember them very clearly many years later. Who can forget the first day at school, college or work? Who can forget receiving a pay-cheque for the first time? Who can forget a first date or a first child? And so we could go on.

At the end of John's Gospel, John wrote *But there are also many other things which Jesus did; were every one of them to be written, I suppose that the world itself could not contain the books that would be written* (John 21:25). Yet all those years later, John's memory of Jesus's attendance at a certain wedding at Cana in Galilee was as vivid in his mind as if it had happened yesterday. How could he ever forget the day when Jesus transformed plain water into the most splendid wine? It was the first miracle Jesus ever performed. John remembered it so well - *This, the first of His signs, Jesus did at Cana in Galilee, and manifested His glory* - and under the influence and guidance of the Holy Spirit (cf John 14:26, 16:13) John selected the incident and recorded it for all time in his wonderful Gospel.

Cana in Galilee was Nathanael's home town, situated a few miles north-east of Nazareth. Let us now, in this chapter, return in our mind's eye to that wedding in Cana - a wedding graced by the presence of the Son of God. Weddings in those days were very lavish occasions. The festivities and feasting did not last for just an afternoon and evening but went on for several days.

> *Since Jesus freely did appear*
> *To grace a marriage feast*
> *O Lord, we ask Thy presence here*
> *Be Thou our glorious guest*

Five points from the *marriage at Cana in Galilee* seem to vie for attention:- 1. The Wedding, 2. The Wine, 3. The Woman, 4. The Wonder, and 5. The Witness.

1. The Wedding

i. Its Timing

On the third day there was a marriage . . .

In those days Jews always married on the third day after the Sabbath - our Tuesday. Interestingly, the first reference to *the third day* in the Bible occurs on its very first page in Genesis 1:13. On this third day of creation we read that at God's command *The earth brought forth vegetation, plants yielding seed according to their own kinds, and trees bearing fruit in which is their seed according to its kind . . .* (Genesis 1:12). This being so, what more fitting day on which to seek the Lord's blessing for a fruitful marriage than the third day? We read of the original third day *And God saw that it was **good*** (Genesis 1:12) - just as we read in Proverbs 18:22 that *He who finds a wife finds a **good** thing and obtains favour from the Lord.* The Bible is clear in its teaching that marriage is good in God's sight . Marriage is a creation ordinance and a divine institution. One man, one woman, 'til death do them part, is God's will and way, and anything which undermines this - for example, adultery, homosexuality, enforced celibacy, polygamy, 'living together' etc - is clearly against both nature and the will of God, and will reap what it sows.

ii. Its Timeliness

Jesus also was invited to the marriage with His disciples . . .

In John 11 we see Jesus comforting the bereaved. In Luke 7:11-17 we see Him sharing in the grief of a funeral. In this incident though we see Him sharing in the joy of a wedding. Jesus really did share our human lot therefore - sin apart. He knows what it is like to be human, and was no stranger to pleasure and pain, sorrow and joy and the daily grind. He wept with those who wept, and here we see Him rejoicing with those who rejoiced.

It was exceedingly fitting for Jesus to be at a wedding, as the Bible describes Jesus as our Heavenly Bridegroom. The Church is the Bride of Christ (Revelation 21:2,9). Christ has betrothed Himself to us in Covenant love – and in response He requires from us our reciprocal love, devotion and faithfulness to Him: *I betrothed you to Christ to present you as a pure bride to her one husband* (2 Corinthians 11:2). *Husbands, love your wives, as Christ loved the Church and gave Himself up for her, that He might sanctify her, having cleansed her by the washing of water with the word* (Ephesians 5:25).

Interestingly, in biblical times marriage had three distinct phases:-

1. The bride was chosen by the groom's father – marriages in those days (as in some countries today) were arranged - the romance came later.
2. The bride was paid for. A sum of money, known as a mohar was given to the bride-to-be's father. This betrothal was now highly binding on both parties.
3. Eventually, and with great ceremony, the bride was taken away by the groom, and they set up their new life together.

So we see 1. The Choice, 2. The Cost, and 3. The Consummation - and these three stages have an exact parallel in Christ's bride the Church:-

1. Our choice. We did not choose Christ but He chose us. The Bible teaches divine election, that *He chose us in Him before the foundation of the world* (Ephesians 1:4).
2. Our cost. Christ came down from heaven to purchase us for God. The cost was priceless because the cost was His own precious blood - *You know that you were ransomed from the futile ways inherited from your fathers, not with perishable things such as silver or gold, but with the precious blood of Christ . . . * (1 Peter 1:18,19).
3. Our consummation. One day Christ will return to collect His bride! This will inaugurate the greatest marriage feast of all time. Revelation 19:9 understates it when it says *Blessed are those who are invited to the marriage supper of the Lamb.*

How fitting and timely therefore for the Bridegroom of our hearts to attend a wedding. The Church is the bride of Christ, and we are His for ever!

From heaven He came and sought her
To be His holy bride
With His own blood He bought her
And for her life He died.

2. The Wine

When the wine gave out, the mother of Jesus said to Him 'they have no wine.'

The wine gave out. Middle eastern wedding festivities lasted several days. When the wine ran out the bridegroom must have been highly embarrassed as it would have been seen as an act of great discourtesy for an eastern host not to provide wine for his guests. The groom was about to be disgraced – the gracious intervention of Jesus apart.

The wine gave out. We can consider this in another way. Have you ever had the experience of having all your earthly wine run out? We can be going on our way quite happily when suddenly the wine of life runs out on us unexpectedly – redundancy strikes, ill-health smites, a cherished relationship is broken, and we are smitten by disappointment, depression and despair. When the wine of life runs out on us we realise just how frail and fragile all this world's seeming joys and pleasures really are. *The things that are seen are transient, but the things that are unseen are eternal* (2 Corinthians 4:18).

It is devastating when our earthly wine gives out - and yet God uses even this to bring blessing to us and glory to Himself, just as He did literally at Cana in Galilee. Our extremity is God's opportunity. He casts us down to lift us up. He runs us dry to fill us full. This is certainly true in our initial Christian experience, as we will only come to faith in Christ when we realise that our wine has run out, and we are hopeless and helpless to save ourselves. Jesus began the Beatitudes by stating *Blessed are the poor in spirit, for theirs is the kingdom of heaven* (Matthew 5:3). Thank the Lord for trials and difficulties if they cast us solely upon Himself. When the wine of life runs out, the truth of the hymn is forced home:-

Fading is the worldling's pleasure
All his boasted pomp and show
Solid joys and lasting treasure
None but Zion's children know.

There is no ultimate joy and satisfaction apart from God. There is no ultimate and lasting joy apart from knowing His salvation in Jesus Christ. Earthly wine does and will run out. God's wine never will, for *in Thy presence there is fullness of joy, in Thy right hand are pleaures for evermore* (Psalm 16:11).

3. The Woman

'O woman, what have you to do with me? My hour has not yet come.'

To our ears this may seem a strange way of addressing one's mother. Some translations paraphrase it in a less harsh way. The *New English Bible,* for example, has 'Your concern mother is not mine.' Comparing Scripture with Scripture though, we know that Jesus had a tender regard for Mary His earthly mother. Even on the cross, whilst He was in absolute agony - as well as having all the elect on His mind - He was concerned for her welfare, and entrusted her to the loving care of the apostle John: *Woman, behold your son . . . Behold your mother! And from that hour the disciple took her to his home* (John 19:26,27).

This being said however, the Bible condemns Roman Catholic 'Mariolatry' completely. No one, not even His mother, had the right to put pressure on Jesus. As the eternal Son of God He could not take directions from anyone, for His commands came only from His Father. Jesus said *I have come in my Father's name* (John 5:43) and *I seek not my own will but the will of Him who sent me* (John 5:30). Mary was not the 'Madonna' of the art of the later Middle Ages. She too was a sinner saved by grace who testified *my spirit rejoices in God my Saviour* (Luke 1:46). She too was subservient to Jesus - as indeed we must be.

O woman. It is a suggestive title. Way back in Eden, when God made the first Gospel promise of a Redeemer, He promised that when the Redeemer came He would be born of a *woman.* He said to the Satan: *I will put enmity between you and the **woman**, between your seed and her seed; He shall bruise your head, and* *you shall bruise His heel* (Genesis 3:15). And in the fullness of time God fulfilled His promise, for *when the time had fully come, God sent forth His Son, born of* **woman**, *born under the law, to redeem those who were under the law, so that we might receive adoption as sons* (Galatians 4:4,5).

Mary then, although only human, gave birth to One who was more than human. She gave birth to the Redeemer! The Holy Spirit enabled her to conceive the eternal Son of God. It is He and not Mary whom we worship, for it is He who has redeemed us by His blood, when His *hour* eventually came.

4. The Wonder

The wonder was the sign. Jesus transformed plain water - water normally used for the Jewish rites of purification - into the most splendid wine. The steward of the feast - an expert in fine wine if ever there was one - was startled that such good wine had been kept for so long. He just did not expect such excellent wine so late on in the feast. How vastly superior is the provision that Jesus makes (both literally and spiritually) to anything which has gone before!

The wonder of *the water now become wine* is the heart of the incident. If we believe in God we will believe in miracles. Here we are dealing with God Himself intervening in His creation, just as elsewhere in John's Gospel we see Jesus multiplying loaves and fishes, giving sight to the blind and raising Lazarus from the dead.

In transforming water into wine Jesus transformed the whole situation. The bridegroom host would never forget it, and neither would John. Wine, in the Bible, is sometimes used as a symbol of cheer: *Thou dost cause . . . plants for man to cultivate, that he may bring forth food from the earth, and wine to gladden the heart of man* (Psalm 104:15).

Who can cheer the heart like Jesus
By His presence all divine?

Jesus transformed water into wine - 120 gallons of it at a conservative estimate. What a lavish picture of abundant grace! He came to give us abundant life (John 10:10). We have seen in the previous chapter how Jesus refused to change stones into bread for Himself - and bread there was a necessity not a luxury. But here He transformed water into wine for others - and wine is a luxury not a necessity. But do we not also see in this incident a picture of what Jesus does for sinners too? Jesus transforms people as well as things, for *If any one is in Christ he is a new creation, the old has passed away, behold, the new has come* (2 Corinthians 5:17).

Here is an interesting consideration concerning this miracle. The first miracle that Jesus did was this one, water into wine. But one of the first miracles Moses performed was similar but different. Moses changed water into blood. Whilst the Israelites were slaves in Egypt, God began to judge Pharoah and the Egyptians. He commanded Aaron to strike the River Nile with his rod *And all the water that was in the Nile turned to blood* (Exodus 7:20). What a contrast there is between Jesus and Moses. It was through Moses that God gave the Law, and we have all broken His Law and as such are under His condemnation. But *Christ redeemed us from the curse of the law* (Galatians 3:13) for Christ is the bringer of grace and mercy. Moses turned water into blood, but Christ turned water into wine. Well does John state in his Prologue in the previous chapter *For the law was given through Moses; grace and truth came through Jesus Christ* (John 1:17). Finally, note:-

5. The Witness

This, the first of His signs, Jesus did at Cana in Galilee, and manifested His glory; and His disciples believed in Him.

The sign pointed to the Saviour, manifesting His glory and eliciting faith in His disciples. Jesus explained of His miracles *the works which the Father has granted me to accomplish, these very works which I am doing, bear me witness that the Father has sent me* (John 5:36). The disciples believed the witness, and John recorded the incident, in keeping with the whole of his book, that we also might believe: *these are written that you may believe that Jesus is the Christ, the Son of God, and that believing you may have life in His name* (John 20:31).

Although this was the first of Jesus's signs, we state reverently that it was not His greatest. The greatest miracle which Jesus performed occured about three years later, when He hung and suffered on a cross, shedding His blood for the sinner's pardon. It may seem contradictory, but Jesus accomplished more by His death than by His life, for His was a transcendant death, availing to save God's elect of all the ages. Even here at Cana we see Jesus under the shadow of the cross. Notice that He said *My hour has not yet come* . The theme can be traced throughout John's Gospel:-

His hour had not yet come (7:30)

His hour had not yet come (8:20)

but in His prayer before His imminent arrest and death, Jesus stated knowingly

Father, the hour has come (17:1).

Chapter 19 of John relates Jesus's *hour* when He died on the cross for our sins, giving up His life as a sinless, spotless sacrifice. It is this *hour* which transforms, not water into wine, but believing sinners into children of God, saved for all eternity. In the words of the ancient love song, these will say to Christ *Your love is better than wine* (Song of Solomon 1:2).

CHAPTER FIVE

The Milestone Of A Famous Feast

Now when Jesus heard this, He withdrew from there in a boat to a
lonely place apart. But when the crowds heard it, they followed Him
on foot from the towns. As He went ashore He saw a great throng;
and He had compassion on them, and healed their sick. When it was
evening, the disciples came to Him and said, 'This is a lonely place,
and the day is now over; send the crowds away to go into the villages
and buy food for themselves.' Jesus said 'They need not go away; you
give them something to eat.' They said to Him, 'We have only five
loaves here and two fish.' And He said, 'Bring them here to me.' Then
He ordered the crowds to sit down on the grass; and taking the five
loaves and the two fish He looked up to heaven, and blessed, and
broke and gave the loaves to the disciples, and the disciples gave them
to the crowds. And they all ate and were satisfied. And they took up
twelve baskets full of the broken pieces left over. And those who ate
were about five thousand men, besides women and children
(Matthew 14:13-20).

There is something lovely about sharing a meal with friends.
The enjoyment is derived not just from the food eaten, but
the company, conversation and camaraderie that goes with
it. This has always been so. In biblical times eating with someone
was symbolic of friendship and fellowship with someone. In Revelation 3:20 we read the risen Christ saying *Behold, I stand at the
door and knock; if any one hears my voice and opens the door, I
will come in to him and eat with him, and he with me.*

Scripture is full of feasts. In Leviticus 23 we read the details
of seven feasts of the Jews - it is as though God commands His

people to be joyful. Then in the New Testament, Jesus Himself said *The kingdom of heaven may be compared to a king who gave a marriage feast for his son* (Matthew 22:2). Christians today often celebrate a simple communion feast, the Lord's Supper, which recalls and appropriates Calvary by faith, in the eating of bread and drinking of wine. The Lord's Supper is itself an anticipation of feasting in heaven - *Blessed are those who are invited to the marriage supper of the Lamb* (Revelation 19:9).

Scripture then is full of feasts. Knowing God is a feast not a fast. Christianity is characterised by plenty not poverty, abundance not abstinence. Jesus said *I came that they may have life and have it abundantly* (John 10:10).

The event known as 'The Feeding of the Five Thousand' (although it would be more accurate to call it 'The Feeding of the Ten Thousand') is yet another special milestone in the earthly life of Christ. This miraculous feast, with Jesus as the host, has much to teach us today. Let us analyse it using seven keys:-
1. The Passage, 2. The People, 3. The Place, 4. The Provider, 5. The Parable, 6. The Provision, and 7. The Purpose.

1. The Passage

The 'Feeding of the Five Thousand' is the only miracle (apart from the Resurrection) recorded by all four Gospel writers. *All Scripture is inspired by God and profitable . . .* (2 Timothy 3:16), and the Holy Spirit in breathing on Matthew, Mark, Luke and John, ensured that they all recorded this amazing picnic independantly -- see Matthew 14:13-20; Mark 6:30-44, Luke 9:10-17 and John 6:1-14. Non-Christians of course will tell you that no miracle occured here, but rather that Jesus just brought out the best in human nature and moved the crowd to share what they had. Such an opinion is contrary to the plain evidence. John records *When the people saw the sign which He had done, they said 'This is indeed the prophet who is to come into the world!' Perceiving then that they were about to come and take Him by force to make*

Him king, Jesus withdrew again to the mountain by Himself (John 6:14,15). The crowd just would not have reacted in such a manner if a genuine miracle had not taken place.

2. The People

The great throng consisted of *about five thousand men, besides women and children* (Matthew 14:21). A conservative estimate therefore would put them at a little over ten thousand. Notice that they were i. A Needy People and ii. A Near People.

i. A Needy People

The need for food is a basic human need. The people felt this need. They had been with Jesus for a long time since their last meal. They were getting hungry by now - and yet they had no food. Their need was thus unmet.

Applying this to the spiritual realm, we may say that just as the universal human experience of physical hunger is desperate if left unmet, so likewise, the universal human experience of spiritual hunger is damnable if left unmet. Rene Paschal the French Philosopher once said 'Every person has a God shaped void in his/her heart, which only God can fill.' Spiritual hunger though is actually healthy. It is a sign of regeneration, because dead people do not experience hunger. Jesus said *Blessed are those who hunger and thirst for righteousness, for they shall be satisfied* (Matthew 5:6). It is only when we are aware of our hunger that we will reach out for God's help. It is only when we realise our plight that we will be receptive to His provision. Just as our physical bodies are kept well by food, so likewise our souls are made well and kept well by faith - faith in Jesus, the Bread of Life.

> *Jesus, Thou joy of loving hearts*
> *Thou Fount of life, Thou light of men*
> *From the best bliss that earth imparts*
> *We turn unfilled to Thee again*

ii. A Near People

The people, although in need, were near to Jesus, the One who could meet their need. They desired to be near Him, for they had heard about His love for needy people. To all those who realise their spiritual need today, we may say confidently that Jesus is very near. Christ is the answer to our every need, and He is only a prayer breath away. The Psalmist wrote *The Lord is near to all who call upon Him, to all who call upon Him in truth. He fulfils the desire of all who fear Him, He also hears their cry and saves them* (Psalm 145:18,19).

3. The Place

Today, on the north east shore of the Sea of Galilee, you can go to a village called Tabgha, and find a church called 'The Church of the Multiplication.' Inside you will see an exquisite loaves and fishes mosaic which commemorates the miracle we are considering. As an artistic commemoration does not necessarily identify the actual location though, we cannot be sure that the miracle happened in the present day Tabgha. A reading of all four accounts suggests that the miracle occurred at Bethsaida ('Fish town') - yet the exact location of Bethsaida is uncertain.

The miracle took place at a 'desert place' (KJV). This must mean a desert-like place, as Mark mentions 'green grass' (Mark 6:39). 'Eremos' is translated variously as 'a lonely place' (RSV) or 'a solitary place' (NIV). The place just could not provide for the people's need as there was nothing life-sustaining in it. The disciples knew this and were all for sending the people away to buy food.

Again, we can apply this spiritually. How is our spiritual hunger to be met? Naturally or supernaturally? Through a poor earthly portion or heaven's potent provision? This world, although it has much to offer us, ultimately just cannot produce the satisfaction our hungry souls crave - any more than that desert-like place could provide satisfaction for the hungry multitudes in Jesus's day. The world cannot satisfy because it is temporal and physical, whereas our souls are eternal and spiritual. *The form of this world is passing away* (1 Corinthians 7:31). *For all that is in the world, the lust of the flesh and the lust of the eyes and the pride of life, is not of the Father but is of the world. And the world passes away and the lust of it; but he who does the will of God abides for ever* (1 John 2:16,17). We see this exemplified in the book of Ecclesiastes. There we read about a man who sought satisfaction through the things of this world - money, fame, power, education, culture - and yet although he had them all he was still unsatisfied. He knew the hollowness of life *under the sun* . *Vanity of vanities, says the Preacher, vanity of vanities! All is vanity* (Ecclesiastes 1:2,3). 'Vanity' has been translated as 'meaningless' and 'a bubble that bursts.' Again we are compelled to state that only Jesus can satisfy the soul.

4. The Provider

The miraculous feeding of more than five hundred people at once reveals three things about Jesus:-

i. His Compassionate Humanity

He had compassion on them (v. 14). Jesus's miracles were always purposeful. They glorified God, they revealed who Jesus was, but they also met the real needs of real people.

The word *compassion* derives from the verb 'spalangomai' in the original Greek. This refers to the entrails of an animal. An impolite translation therefore would say that Jesus had a 'gut reaction.' His inner being was moved with compassion on seeing the people's physical and spiritual need.

It is so good to know in this cold, cruel, confusing world. that Jesus has lost none of His compassion. *Jesus Christ is the same yesterday and today and forever* (Hebrews 13:8). What a Friend we have in Jesus! Friends may fail you, and you may fail your friends. Christians may fail you. The Church may disown you and you may disown the Church, but Jesus never fails! *There is a Friend Who sticks closer than a brother* (Proverbs 18:24).

ii. His Consistent Deity

Only God can do miracles, so Jesus Christ is God. Multiplying loaves and fishes presents no problem to omnipotence - God had been multiplying loaves and fishes long before this time. We cannot do this. I once had a green-fingered Uncle. He was an expert gardener, and yet even he could not give life to a bulb! All he could do was cultivate his garden, leaving God to bring it to life. It is the same in the spiritual realm. *I planted, Apollos watered but God gave the growth* (1 Corinthians 3:6) said Paul. Likewise with cooking. Every boy thinks that his mother is the greatest cook in the world and I am no exception! Yet my mother cannot actually 'produce' a meal. All she can do is take and manipulate the materials which God has already provided, and with the skillful application of heat etc, a meal will result. She can produce a wonderful meal from raw ingredients - yet she cannot produce the raw ingredients. It is the same with evangelism. A preacher cannot manufacture the Bread of Life, all he can do is distribute it. Jesus is the Bread of Life. Evangelism is one beggar showing another where to find bread.

iii. His Creatorial Majesty

The miracle reveals that Jesus is none other than God the Creator. The rest of the Bible is totally in-line with this. *All things were made through Him, and without Him was not anything made that was made* (John 1:3). *For in Him all things were created . . .* (Colossians 1:16). *. . . . one Lord Jesus Christ, through whom are all things* (1 Corinthians 8:6). Never belittle the Person of Christ. The One Who provided a meal for the multidudes by the Sea of Galilee is none less than the uncreated Creator, Jesus Christ the Lord.

5. The Parable

The feeding of the five thousand, of course, is first of all an historical miracle, and not a teaching parable. Yet, with meditation, we can see in this incident an acted, visual parable. (A parable literally means 'to put things side by side').

Note the actions of Jesus when He fed the multitudes – especially the verbs used of Him:- *taking the five loaves and the two fish He looked up to heaven, and blessed* (i.e. He blessed God) *and broke and gave the loaves to the disciples, . . .* (v.19). Taking, blessing, breaking, giving. . .This rings a bell immediately, for in Matthew 26:26 we read *Jesus took bread, and blessed* (God) *and broke it, and gave it to the disciples . . .* The compassion of Christ by the sea therefore points to the communion of Christ at the supper, which in turn points to the cross of Christ at His sacrifice!

At Calvary Christ was taken, broken and given. The cross of Christ is the heart of the Gospel, and is God's full, final and fundamental provision for our spiritual need. *He . . . did not spare His own Son but gave Him up for us all* (Romans 8:32). The cross of Christ is God's eternal, living and life-giving bread which eternally satisfies our spiritual hunger. Jesus said *The bread which I shall give for the life of the world is my flesh* (John 6:51) – and He gave it at Calvary. The verbs applied to the blessed Saviour are taking, blessing, breaking, giving. The verbs appropriate to the believing sinner follow on, they are believing, receiving, eating and living!

Thou art the Bread of Life
Dear Lord to me
Thy holy Word the truth
That saveth me
Give me to eat and live
With Thee above
Teach me to love the truth
For Thou art love

6. The Provision

What would a certain little boy's mother have said on being told that the packed lunch which she had prepared for her son was going to feed more than five thousand people! What a provision!

i. It was a Scriptural Provision

In the Old Testament we read in Exodus 16 and Numbers 11 of God's provision of bread (manna) from heaven for another multitude in another wilderness. This was exactly suited for the Israelite's sustenance – they even received a double portion for the Sabbath day. Just as then, so it is now, Jesus is the Bread of life in this barren, earthly wilderness. He explained to the Jews: *Your fathers ate the manna in the wilderness, and they died . . . I am the living bread which came down from heaven; if any one eats of this bread, he will live for ever . . .* (John 6:49,51).

ii. It was a Sufficient Provision

*They **all** ate and were satisfied . . . they took up twelve baskets left over* (v.20). It was more than sufficient - it was abundant! There was enough left over for a whole basketful for each of the twelve disciples. The disciples were not worthy of it – they were initially all for sending the crowds away. It shows that God is a God of grace. He gives to the undeserving and ill-deserving.

The sufficiency of Christ's provision reminds us of the sufficiency of Christ's propitiation. *He is the proptitiation for our sins, and not for ours only but also for the sins of the whole world* (1 John 2:2). Jesus's work on the cross completely satisfied the claims of divine justice. *It is finished* (John 19:30) He said of it. *For by a single offering He has perfected for all time those who are sanctified* (Hebrews 10:14).

iii. It was a Satisfying Provision

*They all ate and were **satisfied.*** Their hunger was no more. Jesus had provided for them – and He still provides for us. He provides pardon for sin, peace with God and the promise of a home in glory for all who believe in Him. There is no ultimate satisfaction apart from God's provision in Jesus Christ. Augustine said 'Lord, Thou hast made us for Thyself, and our hearts are restless until they find their rest in Thee' – and he was right.

iv. It was a Suggestive Provision

How did Jesus feed the crowds? Did He command bread from heaven to fall down upon them directly? He could have, but He chose not to. Matthew 14:19 says He *gave the loaves to the disciples and the disciples gave them to the multitudes.* How suggestive. The incident is a lesson of what God does for us, to be sure. But is it not also a lesson of what God can do *through* us too? *Loaves . . . disciples . . . multitudes.* Who knows just how God can use even our humble loaves and fishes when they are dedicated to Him. Thank God that He uses ordinary people to accomplish His extra-ordinary purposes.

7. The Purpose

We have already alluded to the fact that Jesus's miracles were for a distinctive purpose. John terms His miracles 'signs,' and signs always point beyond and away from themselves. The signs reveal the Saviour. The purpose of this sign was simple. It not only met human need, but it authenticated Jesus's claim. In John 6:35 Jesus claimed *I am the bread of life. He who comes to me shall not hunger, and he who believes in me shall never thirst.* Jesus truly is the living and life-giving bread, and Jesus alone. Seeking satisfaction in anything or anyone else other than Jesus is living on a synthetic substitute, and eventually will be shown to be so. The message of the milestone of the miracle of the 'feeding of the five thousand' is this: Jesus is the Bread of Life and only Jesus can satisfy the soul.

Break Thou the Bread of Life
Dear Lord to me
As Thou didst break the bread
Beside the sea.
Beyond the sacred page
I seek Thee, Lord
My spirit pants for Thee
O living Word.

CHAPTER SIX

The Milestone Of Peter's Declaration

Now when Jesus came into the district of Caesarea Philippi, He asked His disciples, 'Who do men say that the Son of Man is?' And they said, 'Some say John the Baptist, others say Elijah, and others Jeremiah or one of the prophets.' He said to them, 'But who do you say that I am?' Simon Peter replied, 'You are the Christ, the Son of the living God.' And Jesus answered him, 'Blessed are you Simon Bar-Jona! For flesh and blood has not revealed this to you, but my Father who is in heaven. And I tell you, you are Peter, and on this rock I will build my church, and the gates of Hades shall not prevail against it. I will give you the keys of the kingdom of heaven, and whatever you bind on earth shall be bound in heaven, and whatever you loose on earth shall be loosed in heaven.' Then He strictly charged the disciples to tell no one that He was the Christ.

From that time Jesus began to show His disciples that He must go to Jerusalem and suffer many things from the elders and chief priests and scribes, and be killed, and on the third day be raised. And Peter took Him and began to rebuke Him, saying, 'God forbid, Lord! This shall never happen to you.' But He turned and said to Peter, 'Get behind me, Satan! You are a hindrance to me; for you are not on the side of God, but of men' (Matthew 16:13-23).

We can all trace distinct turning points in our lives when we look back over our years. Major and minor happenings can affect our whole course and direction. Opting for one subject in preference to another at school, for instance, can, with hindsight, be seen as a turning point, for such a choice affected our whole career. Then there are seemingly 'chance' occurrences which, with hindsight, led to meeting one's spouse or perhaps a change of career direction and location. Then there are the major tragedies and calamities - as well as the ecstatic joys - which change our whole outlook upon life, putting things into a different perspective. Many Christians can name the time and place of their conversion, and what a turning point in life is conversion. The Christian, of course, does not believe that these milestones and turning points are by 'chance,' for he is able to say to God *My times are in Thy hand* (Psalm 31:15), knowing He has foreordained everything that comes to pass.

In considering Peter's declaration at Caesarea Philippi, we come to a distinct turning point in the earthly life of Jesus:-

> 'The confession by Peter of Jesus' Messiahship is in many ways the turning-point of the Synoptic Gospels, because it is from this point that the shadow of the cross falls over the ministry'
> *(The New Bible Commentary Revised,* p.836).

A comparison of two verses in Matthew brings this juncture out quite sharply. Matthew 4:17 reads *From that time Jesus began to preach saying 'Repent, for the kingdom of heaven is at hand.'* Matthew 16:21 however reads *From that time Jesus began to show His disciples that He must go to Jerusalem and suffer many things . . . and be killed, and on the third day be raised.*

Needless to say, this event at Caesarea Philippi is no fable. Each Synoptic Gospel writer ensured it was included in his particular Gospel (see Matthew 16:13-23; Mark 8:31 ff and Luke 9:18 ff). Even today, if you had the time and means, you could go to the land of Israel. There, in the northern Galilee district, at the foot of Mount Hermon and the source of the River Jordan, you will find a village called Banias. If you read the account of Peter's declaration there, you will be reading amidst the very scenery in which the events described occurred.

1. The Pertinent Question

Who do men say that the Son of Man is? . . . Who do you say that I am?

The ministry of Jesus made such an impact that all sorts of opinions concerning His identity were proferred. The question 'Who do you say that I am?' transcends the moment in which it was originally asked. The question is crucially relevant today and always will be so, for our attitude to Jesus actually determines where we spend eternity (even though primarily eternity is determined by His attitude to us). Our answers to questions are often determinitive – if you have ever sat an examination, or attended a job interview you will know what I mean. Our answers to questions certainly affect our lives. But our answer to the question *Who do you say that I am?* affects our eternity. It is the most vital, crucial and pertinent question we will ever be asked – and no one else can answer the question for us. John Newton brought this out well in the following lines:-

'What think ye of Christ?' is the test
To try both your state and your scheme
You cannot be right in the rest
Unless you think rightly of Him
As Jesus appears in your view –
As He is beloved or not
So God is disposed to you
And mercy or wrath is your lot.

2. Peter's Confession

Simon Peter replied 'You are the Christ, the Son of the living God.'

How plain, clear and unmistakable was Peter's reply. Paraphrasing it, we can hear him say "To this straight question I will give my honest answer. I have lived with you for a while now Jesus. I have seen your works of power and heard your words of life. This being so, I have no option but to confess that You are the long awaited Messiah." *You are the Christ.* 'Despite foreshadowings (especially 14:33) this is the first considered affirmation of such faith in Jesus' *(The New Bible Commentary Revised,* p.837). Peter never recanted this confession and profession. His conviction if anything grew stronger the older he got. On the day of Pentecost he did not hesitate to proclaim to a great crowd: *Let all the house of Israel therefore know assuredly that God has made Him both Lord and Christ, this Jesus whom you crucified* (Acts 2:36).

Peter's confession is clarified even more when we consider something of the history of the place in which it was made, Caesarea Philippi. Caesarea Philippi was steeped in history:-

At Caesarea Philippi, Herod the Great had built a large marble temple to Caesar Augustus - Augustus had actually given the town to Herod as a gift. Later, Philip the Tetrarch (Herod's son) renamed the town Caesarea Philippi to (egotistically) distinguish it from the Caesarea on the coast. The town was therefore built as a monument in honour of an earthly, temporal emperor and king. Peter's confession of Christ here therefore acknowledged Christ not so much as an earthly king (although He is and will be that) but as an eternal King! It acknowledged Christ as a greater than Caesar. It acknowledged Him as 'Great David's Greater Son,' the Anointed One of God Who had come to bring in the Kingdom of Heaven.

In Old Testament times, Baal, the infamous fertility god was worshipped in the Caesarea Philippi district. Later, the Greeks substituted their god Pan for Baal, and the town took the name Paneas, in being a shrine to Pan. Here though, Peter confesses Jesus as *the Son of the living God.* It is as though he is telling us that all other gods are idols. Jesus Christ is the Son of God and God the Son. There is no other. He is the Son of the living God, and He alone can give eternal life. There was no life to be had in the life-less ancient gods of Baal and Pan, just as there is no life to be had in the modern gods of money, materialism, education, sex, 'isms' and movements. Jesus Christ is the Son of the living God.

He is the way and the truth and the life (John 14:6). He alone can give eternal life to guilty, dying, hell-deserving sinners for *the free gift of God is eternal life in Christ Jesus our Lord* (Romans 6:23).

3. The Paternal Revelation

Blessed are you, Simon Bar Jona! For flesh and blood has not revealed this to you but my Father who is in heaven . . .

Note the benediction: *Blessed are you.* Knowing Jesus is the only lasting blessing, for knowing Jesus is eternal life (John 17:3). *The blessing of the Lord makes rich and He adds no sorrow with it* (Proverbs 10:22). Note too though that this benediction was the result not of human reasoning but of divine revelation: *Flesh and blood* (i.e. human nature)*has not revealed this* (i.e. knowledge of Myself) *to you but my Father who is in heaven.*

It is exceedingly humbling when we realise that we are totally dependant upon God for our salvation. Salvation is tri-une. It is only when the Spirit of God reveals to us our desparate plight, and enables us to know and trust in the Son of God that we will be reconciled to God the Father. We could never work or work-out our own salvation apart from the tri-une work of God the Father, Son and Holy Spirit accomplishing salvation for us and applying salvation to us and working salvation in us.

Consider all that Peter had seen to date: the crowds astonishment at Jesus's authority as He concluded the Sermon on the Mount (Matthew 7:28,29); Jesus's cleansing of a leper at a touch (Matthew 8:1 ff); His forgiving and consequent healing of a paralysed man (Matthew 8:1 ff); His miraculous feeding of five thousand plus (Matthew 14:13 ff); His enabling of Peter himself to defy the laws of nature and walk on the sea (Matthew 14:28 ff). . . The evidence was all there, but Peter only came to realise just Who Jesus was because of a divine work of grace in his heart. And it is the same today. The evidence for the deity of Christ is all there in the Bible. It is irrefutable - or is it? Many are not convinced, will not be convinced, or are not really bothered. Why? Because they have not had (or not yet had) a personal experience of God's particular grace, when by His Holy Spirit He brings them alive to Himself, convicting them of sin and converting them to Christ. We are powerless to convert ourselves. *It is the Spirit that gives life, the flesh is of no avail* (John 6:63). *God has revealed to us through the Spirit* (1 Corinthians 1:10). Salvation is a result of being re-born *not of blood nor of the will of the flesh nor of the will of man, but of God* (John 1:13).

4. The Promised Edification

And I tell you, you are Peter, and on this rock I will build my church, and the gates of hades will not prevail against it.

The Church is the property and possession of Jesus Christ - *my church.* It consists of all who are united to Him by saving faith. His Church is made up of living stones, sinners saved by grace, founded on the Rock Christ Jesus. Jesus is building His Church! When the final living stone is put in place He will come again and receive the Church to Himself.

Notice the security of the 'church building.' *The gates of hades will not prevail against it.* Nothing can hinder or thwart Christ's building programme. God has His elect. Christ died for these elect. The Holy Spirit will draw in these elect and build the Church. No natural or supernatural power can spoil Christ's Church.

Gates of hell shall never 'gainst the Church prevail,
We have Christ's own promise, and that cannot fail.

'The gates suggest the picture of a fortress or prison which lock in the dead and lock out their rescuers. This would imply that the church is on the offensive, and its Master will plunder the domain of Satan'
(*The New Bible Commentary Revised,* p.837).

In Genesis 22:17 God promised to Abraham *your descendants shall possess the gate of their enemies.*

It is admitted that the verse we are considering has been the source of much controversy. Some have used it to deny that there ever was a Church until Pentecost. Others have used (or mis-used) the verse to teach the supposed infallibility of the Pope of Rome. Let us take up these two controversies:-

i.   Dispensationalists teach that the Church did not begin until Pentecost.

John Murray refutes this most ably:-

> It is necessary to distinguish between the form of the visible church under the Old Testament and its form under the New. Such a distinction is implied in the words of our Lord to Peter: 'Thou art Peter, and upon this rock I will build my church; and the gates of hell shall not prevail against it' (Matthew 16:18). Jesus was referring to the new form which the church was to assume in consequence of his own messianic work. He calls it 'my church'. Full allowance must be made for the new form of structure and administration established by the death, resurrection and ascension of Christ and the outpouring of the Holy Spirit at Pentecost. *Nevertheless the distinction does not warrant the denial of the existence of the church under the Old Testament, nor the generic unity and continuity of the church in both dispensations* (italics mine). In addition to the fact that the organisation of the people of God in the Old Testament is expressly called the church (Acts 7:38), we must bear in mind that the church in the New Testament is founded upon the covenant made with Abraham. The specific covenant administration under which the New Testament church operates is the extension and unfolding of the Abrahamic covenant. This is distinctly the argument of the Apostle Paul in the epistle to the Galatians when he says, 'they which be of faith are blessed with faithful

Abraham ...' It is this basic and underlying unity of the covenant of grace and of promise that establishes the generic unity and continuity of the church. In terms of covenant union and communion the church is but the covenant people of God in all ages and among all nations. The promise which epitomises the unity, and which summarises the constitutive principle of the church is, 'I will be their God, and they shall be my people.' '

ii. Then what of the claims of the Church of Rome which teaches that as 'the rock' supposedly refers to Peter, the Church (or rather their church) is founded upon Peter, with the Pope as Peter's successor?

The 'rock' does not refer to Peter but to Peter's Saviour. 'The Church's one foundation is Jesus Christ her Lord.' The Greek brings this out more clearly than the English. 'You are Petros (a little pebble) and upon this Petra (great rock) I will build my church.' Peter, of course, was a great Apostle, but until his dying day he was a sinner saved by grace. In denying His Lord three times he would be the first to admit just what an unstable foundation he was on which to build the Church! Peter was unstable and impetous. He once had to be corrected by Paul at Antioch for not practising what he preached (Galatians 2:11). The Rock and Foundation of the Church can only be Jesus Christ. *No other foundation can any one lay than that which is laid, which is Christ Jesus* (1 Corinthians 3:11). In his first letter Peter himself referred to Jesus as being the rock – *A stone that will make men stumble, a rock that will make them fall* (1 Peter 2:8). Jesus is the rock on which the Church is being built. He is building His Church as you read, and it is indestructable:-

> *On the Rock of Ages founded*
> *What can shake thy sure repose?*
> *With salvation's walls surrounded*
> *Thou may'st smile at all thy foes.*

5. The Pentecostal Proclamation

I will give you the keys of the kingdom of heaven, and whatever you bind on earth shall be bound in heaven, and whatever you loose on earth shall be loosed in heaven.

This verse is more understandable when we consider it against its original middle-eastern background. If you have ever seen the vast gates of a middle-eastern city (the Damascus Gate in Jerusalem, for example) you will undertand easily how a key symbolises power and authority. A key could both let people into a city, and a key could lock people out. The verse has echoes in both testaments: *I will place on his shoulder the key of the house of David; he shall open and none shall shut and he shall shut and none shall open* (Isaiah 22:22) and in Revelation 3:7 Jesus is referred to as *the holy one, the true one, who has the key of David, who opens and none shall shut, who shuts and no one opens.*

The *New Bible Dictionary* explains:

> 'The power of the keys is the phrase used to describe the authority given by our Lord to His disciples . . . It is a power which may be said to operate. . . by preaching the gospel the kingdom of God is opened to believers and shut to the impenitent . . .
> 'Since it is the doctrine of the gospel that opens heaven to us, it is beautifully expressed by the metaphorical appellation of "keys". Binding and loosing are simply nothing other than the preaching and application of the gospel' (Luther)' (p.956).

In Acts chapter 2 we see Peter wielding the keys of the kingdom in a mighty way. There, on the day of Pentecost, he preached Christ, and three thousand believed his message and were freed from the bondage of sin and entered through the gates of the kingdom of heaven. Reading on through the thrilling book of Acts, on almost every page we see the apostles opening up the kingdom of heaven to believers using the mighty key of preaching. And it is just the same today. People today enter into the kingdom of heaven when they respond to the preaching of the Gospel and put their faith in the Saviour – but more formidably, people today also seal their own doom when they hear about Christ but turn Him away. It is amazing to think that Almighty God wields His authority today through His preachers. No man has ultimate authority. All authority is derived from God, and yet divine authority is exercised through feeble, fallible men, when they faithfully preach the Gospel. The preached Gospel is still *the power of God for salvation to every one who has faith* (Romans 1:16), *the word of the cross . . . to us who are being saved it is the power of God* (1 Corinthians 1:18).

6. The Pending Crucifixion

From that time Jesus began to show His disciples that He MUST go to Jerusalem and suffer many things . . . and be killed, and on the third day be raised.

Whilst Jesus did not deny Peter's confession of Him as Messiah, almost immediately He took great care to define the exact nature of His Messiahship. Unlike the great pomp and show associated with an earthly king's temple in Caesarea Philippi, this King was to be a suffering King. The Gospel is described by Paul in terms of *the folly of what we preach* (1 Corinthians 1: 21), and the unbelieving world then as now just could not make sense of a suffering Messiah. Yet it was through His suffering that Christ opened the kingdom of heaven for all believers. The cross of Christ was no accident but an appointment. Its necessity was known only too well by Jesus, and He revealed its necessity to His disciples here at Caesarea Philippi. *He MUST go to Jersualem and suffer ...* The scriptural promises of a suffering Messiah had to be fulfilled (see Psalm 22 and Isaiah 53 et al). Jesus could thus say before He died that *The Son of Man goes as it is written of Him* (Matthew 26:24), and the early Christian Creed could define *Christ died for our sins in accordance with the Scriptures* (1 Corinthians 15:3).

We have seen in earlier chapters how Jesus lived constantly under the shadow of the cross - even before He breathed His first earthly breath this was so. In the Bible, all roads lead to Calvary, and here, at the turning point of Caesarea Philippi the cross came into sharper focus when Peter confessed Jesus to be the longed for Christ.

Near the cross! O Lamb of God
Bring its scenes before me
Help me walk from day to day
With its shadow oe'r me

In the cross, in the cross
Be my glory ever
Till my ransomed soul shall find
Rest beyond the river

CHAPTER SEVEN

The Milestone Of His Transfiguration

Now about eight days after these sayings He took with Him Peter and John and James, and went up on the mountain to pray. And as He was praying, the appearance of His countenance was altered, and His raiment became dazzling white. And behold, two men talked with Him, Moses and Elijah, who appeared in glory and spoke of His departure, which He was to accomplish at Jerusalem. Now Peter and those who were with Him were heavy with sleep, and when they wakened they saw His glory and the two men who stood with Him. And as the men were parting from Him, Peter said to Jesus, 'Master, it is well that we are here; let us make three booths, one for you and one for Moses and one for Elijah' – not knowing what he said. As he said this, a cloud came and overshadowed them; and they were afraid as they entered the cloud. And a voice came out of the cloud, saying, 'This is my Son, my Chosen; listen to Him!' And when the voice had spoken, Jesus was found alone. And they kept silence and told no one in those days anything of what they had seen (Luke 9:28-36).

The description of the land of Israel as *a land of hills and valleys* (Deuteronomy 11:11) could be a description of life itself too. As we live out our days we experience many hills and valleys, or highs and lows - the majority of the time being lived on a routine, ordinary and mundane level. We all have our 'highs' to relate, but also our devastating 'lows'. It may be that we need the valleys to appreciate the hills.

The transfiguration of the Lord Jesus Christ brings us literally and spiritually to one of the highlights of His earthly life. It was literally a mountain-top experience, occurring on Mount Hermon, some 2,814 m above sea level. The event marks a prominent mile-stone in the life of Jesus. All three Gospel writers record it (see Matthew 17:1-8; Mark 9:2-8 and Luke 9:28-36) and John seems to allude to it in his Prologue where he testifies *we have beheld His glory, glory as of the only Son from the Father* (John 1:14). The event made such an impact on Peter, that many years later, as an old man nearing his death, he still remembered as clear as day how *we were eyewitnesses of His majesty. For when He received honour and glory from God the Father and the voice was borne to Him by the majestic glory, 'This is my beloved Son, with whom I am well pleased,' we heard this voice borne from heaven, for we were with Him on the holy mountain* (2 Peter 1:17,18).

The transfiguration of the Lord Jesus Christ, is infinitely greater than human words can tell, so any attempted 'explanation' of it should be approached with the utmost reverence and care, aware of the limitations that there are when finite, sinful humanity tries to comprehend infinite, holy Deity. Bearing this in mind though, let us climb the holy mountain with the Apostles and see:-

1. Jesus Christ: The Pre-eminent Son of God
2. Jesus Christ: The Promise of the Scriptures of God
3. Jesus Christ: The Procurer of the Salvation of God

1. Jesus Christ: The Pre-eminent Son of God

the appearance of His countenance was altered, and His raiment became dazzling white . . . they saw His glory . . .

i. The Vision of Glory

In a day of 'comparative religion' various religions and phi-losophies are put side by side and discussed. The Transfiguration however teaches us that we dare not bring the Lord Jesus Christ into the discussion, for here we are not dealing with the compara-tive but with the incomparative - the Incomparable Son of God. Jesus cannot even be put into the same 'booth' as Moses and Elijah, great men though they were. Here we are not dealing with 'religion' - man's feeble attempt to find God. Rather, the transformed appearance of the Lord Jesus, along with the dazzling garments of heavenly glory, make us shut our mouths and fall on our knees. Here we are in the Royal Presence. The Kingdom of God is in our midst. We are driven to fear, reverence, repentance, worship and awe as we stand on this holy ground, made holy by the presence of Holiness Himself. Justly does James describe Him as *our Lord Jesus Christ, the Lord of glory* (James 2:1).

ii. The Voice of God

The juxtaposition of the Transfiguration just a week or so after Caesarea Philippi is striking. At Caesarea Philippi we saw how Jesus asked *Who do men say that I am?* Here though we have a testimony infinitely greater than any mere human opinion. At the Transfiguration God Himself spoke from heaven and testified to His Son, giving the divine answer as to Jesus' identity: *And a voice came out of the cloud, saying 'This is my Son, my Chosen; listen to Him'* (Luke 9:35). Needless to say *God is not man, that He should lie* (Numbers 23:19). Jesus Christ is the Son of God and God the Son. The transfigured vision reveals it, and the testifying Voice proclaims it.

iii. The Verity of Greatness

On the Mount of Transfiguration we are privileged to glimpse nothing less than something of the preincarnate glory of the Lord Jesus Christ. He made reference to the *glory which I had with Thee before the world was made* (John 17:5) and we glimpse something of it here. From a reading of the account of the Transfiguration then, how can we ever again consider and countenance the popular view that Jesus is a mere man and founder of the Christian religion? Never! *He reflects the glory of God and bears the very stamp of His nature* (Hebrews 1:2). *He is the image of the invisible God* (Colossians 1:15). When words lose their coinage,

Jesus alone can be described as truly 'great'. Justly is and has He been worshipped by the Christian community in the words of the *Te Deum:* THOU ARE THE KING OF GLORY O CHRIST, THOU ART THE EVERLASTING SON OF THE FATHER.

2. Jesus Christ: The Promise of the Scriptures of God

Who should join Jesus and the three frightened Apostles on the Mount but *Moses and Elijah* (v.30).

The *New Bible Dictionary* under the heading 'Transfiguration' explains:-

> 'There are many features about the account which derive significance from the OT. Moses and Elijah represent the Law and the Prophets witnessing to the Messiah and being fulfilled and superseded by Him. Each of them had had a vision of the glory of God on a mountain, Moses on Sinai (Exodus 24:15) and Elijah on Horeb (1 Kings 19:8). Each of them left no known grave (Deuteronomy 34:6; 2 Kings 2:11). The law of Moses and the coming of Elijah are mentioned together in the last verses of the OT (Malachi 4:4-6). The two men at the empty tomb (Luke 24:4; John 20:12) and at the ascension (Acts 1:10) and the 'two witnesses' (Revelation 11:3) are sometimes also identified with Moses and Elijah. The heavenly voice . . . marks Jesus out not only as the Messiah but also as the Prophet of Deuteronomy 18:15 ff.'

Moses and Elijah represent the Law and the Prophets respectively. Jesus said *Think not that I have come to abolish the law and the prophets; I have not come to abolish them but to fulfil them* (Matthew 5:17) and after His resurrection, on the Emmaus road we read that *beginning with Moses and all the prophets, He interpreted to them in all the Scriptures the things concerning Himself* (Luke 24:27). Jesus is the one grand theme of the symphony of Scripture, as we shall see.

Jesus and Moses

Moses was not permitted to enter the promised land - or was he? Here, about 1300 years later He was standing on the soil of Israel with the blessed King of Israel.

Under God, Moses authored the first five books of the Bible, the Torah. Jesus said that *If you believed Moses, you would believe me, for he wrote of me* (John 5:46). Moses certainly did write about Jesus, for in the first five books of the Bible, we see Jesus as:-

> The promised Seed of the woman who will crush the serpent's head (Genesis 3:15)
>
> The Ark of Refuge, who delivers us from the wrath to come (Genesis 6)
>
> The Seed of Abraham, in whom the whole world would be blessed (Genesis 12)
>
> The antitype of the ram, sacrificed in the stead of Isaac (Genesis 22)
>
> The antitype of Joseph, rejected, humiliated, exalted, needed and worshipped (Genesis 40 ff)
>
> The Passover Lamb, whose blood, when applied personally, saves from the fearful angel of death when he passes over our house (Exodus 12)
>
> The One Perfect Sacrifice, fulfilling the burnt, cereal, sin, trespass and peace offerings of Leviticus 1–7.
>
> The antitype of the bronze serpent which Moses lifted up in the wilderness, for in looking to Him lifted up, we have eternal life (Numbers 25:17, cf John 3:14,15)
>
> The Prophet of Deuteronomy 18:18, for Jesus is the Word made flesh. Listen to Him!

It was through Moses that God gave the Law at Mount Sinai. The moral law of the Ten Commandments is bad news for us, as it reveals our sin; and yet it is good news if it drives us to Christ for justification. Christ fulfilled the law in our stead, and on the cross bore the penalty of the broken law in our place. *Christ redeemed us from the curse of the law* . . . (Galatians 3:13). Whilst the law condemns us, the Christian need not fear for *There is therefore now no condemnation for those who are in Christ Jesus* (Romans 8:1). Paul goes as far as to say that *Christ is the end of the law that everyone who has faith may be justified* (Romans 10:4). If we are Christ's, amazingly, God sees us 'in' Him - fully righteous in relation to the law and with Himself.

Jesus and Elijah

Elijah is a man of such stature that he deserves a whole book to himself. The Old Testament taught that Elijah would return to earth as a forerunner of the Messiah (Malachi 4:5). John the Baptist paved the way for Jesus in a very Elijah-like manner, but here we have the man himself, a prince among prophets, standing with The Prophet and fulfilment of all prophecy. Jesus certainly is the fulfilment of all prophecy, as the following 'whistle-stop tour' of the Old Testament prophets will show:-

> In *Isaiah* we see Jesus as the Suffering Servant of God, bearing the sins of many, in one of the clearest pictures of Calvary in the whole Bible (Isaiah 53).
> In *Jeremiah* we see Jesus as the Mediator of the New Covenant between God and His people, through whom God is able to forgive and forget our sins (Jeremiah 31).
> In *Lamentations* we see Jesus's innermost heart made bare as He hangs on the Cross: *Is it nothing to you all you who pass by* . . . (Lamentations 1:12).
> In *Daniel* we see Jesus as the stone cut without hands, coming to set up His universal Kingdom; Daniel's famous 'Seventy weeks' prophecy even mentions the Christ being 'cut off' in Jerusalem (Daniel 9:26).
> In *Hosea* we are moved by God's steadfast love for His unfaithful Israel, just as Christ loved the Church, His body and bride, and gave Himself up for her.

In *Joel* we witness the Holy Spirit of Jesus being poured out on the day of Pentecost.

In *Amos* we read of the rebuilding of the fallen booth of David, quoted in Acts 15:16,17 as referring to the time when Jesus will gather the Gentiles into His fold.

In *Obadiah* we see a prediction of the coming Kingdom of the Lord, reminding us that 'Jesus shall reign where'er the sun, does his successive journeys run.'

In *Jonah* we read how *Jonah was in the belly of the fish three days and three nights* (1:17), quoted by Jesus Himself in reference to His death and resurrection (Matthew 12:40).

In *Micah* 5:2 we have a prophecy of the exact location of Christ's birth, Bethlehem. We saw in chapter one how this was fulfilled against all odds.

Nahum's name means 'comfort.' Only Jesus can bring the comfort of God to us. He Himself actually ministered in Caper Nahum, the village of Nahum.

Habbakuk announces *the just shall live by faith* (2:4). He was a good Protestant! We have no right relationship with God apart from faith in Jesus Christ.

Zephaniah majors on the coming Day of the Lord. The New Testament likewise tells of the return of the Prince of Peace, when the kingdom of this world will become the kingdom of our Lord and of His Christ.

Haggai was the prophet of the rebuilding of the temple, and speaks of the greater splendour that the house of God would have in the latter days. In John 2 Jesus spoke of the temple of His body - and what surpassing splendour this temple had here on the Mount of Transfiguration.

Zechariah foretold both the time when the Messiah would ride into Jerusalem on a lowly ass, and of a fountain for sin and uncleanness. The New Testament proclaims that it is the blood of Jesus which cleanses us from all sin (1 John 1:7) and

Malachi tells us of the Sun of Righteousness which would arise with healing in His wings. Along with Wesley, we take this as a reference to none other than the Lord Jesus Christ.

And so we see how Jesus is indeed the promise of the Scriptures of God. Peter in his final letter said *we have the prophetic word made more sure* (2 Peter 1:19). Revelation 19:10 *For the testimony of Jesus is the spirit of prophecy.* The Old Testament without its New Testament fulfilment in Christ is like an unfinished sentence or an unfulfilled longing, *for all the promises of God find their 'Yes' in Him* (2 Corinthians 1:20). Having taken something of an Emmaus walk, let us now see what the stupendous transfiguration teaches us about

3. Jesus Christ: The Procurer of the Salvation of God

When Jesus conversed with Moses and Elijah on the Mount of Transfiguration, the conversation was exceedingly to the point. *They spoke of His departure which He was to accomplish at Jerusalem* (Luke 9:31). This is very much in line with the whole of Dr Luke's Gospel, as the whole of Luke's book has a compass which, instead of pointing North points to Jerusalem, and the death of Christ outside her city walls. Luke has twenty four chapters in his book, and as early as Luke 9:51 we read that *Jesus set His face to go to Jerusalem.* Calvary was never far from Christ's mind. Luke records Him saying *I have a baptism to be baptised with; and how I am constrained until it is accomplished* (Luke 12:50).

Mr Jim Flanigan's article 'His Transfiguration' in the May/June edition of the *Assembly Testimony* of 1994 brings out the contrast between the Mount of Transfiguration and 'mount' Calvary with great insight:-

> 'It is most instructive, and touching too, to compare this mount of glory with Golgotha. Behold His countenance, His face, here shining as the sun transfigured. At Golgotha it was marred more than any man's, disfigured. Here on the Holy Mount the darkness of night was turned to day. At Calvary the brightness of the noonday was turned to darkness. Daylight became midnight on the mount of suf-

fering. 'Let us make three tabernacles', says Peter, on the mount of glory. But three crosses awaited on the other mount of sorrow. Two men appeared with Him on the Holy Mount, Moses and Elijah, and spake of His decease. Two men, thieves, hung by His side on the mount where He died. From the opened heaven, at the transfiguration there came a voice, 'My beloved Son.' At Calvary heaven was closed and silent, and the Saviour cries 'My God, my God.' On the Holy Mount His garments shone white and glistering in the glory. At Golgotha they stripped Him and gambled for His garments at the foot of His cross. In the sacred record, the transfiguration precedes the crucifixion, but it is, in fact, a preview of the glory that was to follow. As has been remarked by another, 'When the Son began to witness concerning His sufferings (Matthew 16:21), the Father witnessed concerning His glory (2 Peter 1:17). He who was to be put to shame by men received honour and glory from the Father' (p.68).

i. A Departure is Announced

They spoke of *His departure*. The word for departure is 'exodus.' This takes us back to the central event of the Old Testament, the Exodus, when Israel was delivered from cruel slavery in Egypt through the shed blood of the passover lamb. John the Baptist said of Christ *Behold, the Lamb of God who takes away the sin of the world* (John 1:29). Jesus delivers from a worse slavery than Egypt. He delivers us from the penalty and power of sin, enabling us to walk in freedom and fellowship with our Maker.

ii. A Deliverance is Accomplished

They spoke of His departure which He was to accomplish at Jerusalem. Jesus really did procure salvation at Jerusalem when He died on the cross. Calvary was a divine work. God the Father was fully satisfied with this work, and accepts all who trust in

Christ on the basis of it. *In Him we have redemption through His blood, the forgiveness of our trespasses according to the riches of His grace* (Ephesians 1:7). The finished work of Christ brings much assurance to the believing soul. All doubt will vanish instantly when we look away from ourselves and look to Jesus, the author and finisher of our faith (cf Hebrews 12:2). We do not work to accomplish our own salvation, rather we trust in the salvation already accomplished for us by Christ's finished work. On the cross He declared *It is finished* (John 19:30), and the matchless Psalm of Calvary ends saying how men shall *proclaim His deliverance to a people yet unborn, that He has wrought it* (Psalm 22:31).

And so, with reluctance, we leave the Mount of Transfiguration. It was one of the highlights of Jesus's earthly life, but did not last for long. We are soon brought down to earth in the scene following. The next scene brings us face to face with an epileptic boy and the unbelief of the disciples (Matthew 17:14-20) – but we said at the outset that life is composed of the hills and the valleys, the highs and the lows. Monday morning follows on from Sunday evening worship. Bills, nappies, headaches, disappointments, signing on the dole etc etc are as much part and parcel of life as the highlights. But knowing Christ makes a difference to them all. The same Christ encountered on the Mount of Transfiguration also walks with us here in the valley below, transfiguring our lives and situations.

> *'Tis good Lord to be here!*
> *Thy glory fills the night*
> *Thy face and garments like the sun*
> *Shine with unborrowed light*
>
> *'Tis good Lord to be here!*
> *Yet we may not remain*
> *But since Thou bidst us leave the mount*
> *Come with us to the plain.*

CHAPTER EIGHT

The Milestone Of Gethsemane

And they went to a place which is called Gethsemane; and He said to His disciples, 'Sit here, while I pray.' And He took with Him Peter and James and John, and began to be greatly distressed and troubled. And He said to them 'My soul is very sorrowful, even to death; remain here, and watch.' And going a little farther, He fell on the ground and prayed that, if it were possible, the hour might pass from Him. And He said, 'Abba, Father, all things are possible to Thee; remove this cup from me; yet not what I will, but what Thou wilt.' And He came and found them sleeping, and He said to Peter, 'Simon, are you asleep? Could you not watch one hour? Watch and pray that you may not enter into temptation; the spirit indeed is willing, but the flesh is weak.' And again He went away and prayed, saying the same words. And again He came and found them sleeping, for their eyes were very heavy; and they did not know what to answer Him. And He came the third time, and said to them, 'Are you still sleeping and taking your rest? It is enough; the hour has come; the Son of man is betrayed into the hands of sinners. Rise, let us be going; see, my betrayer is at hand' (Mark 14:32-42).

In reading the account of the 'Agony in Gethsemane' we are treading upon familiar soil. The incident is well known and seems to have permeated many Christian prayers and hymns.

Garden of gloom appalling
Where, in His sore amaze
Earthward in anguish falling
Prostrate, the Saviour prays
Prays in exceeding sorrow
Prays, on the ground bowed low
Facing the dark tomorrow
Full of unfathomed woe

In this chapter we are going to obey the injunction of another hymn when it exhorts:-

> *Go to Gethsemane, my soul*
> *And watch with Jesus there*
> *Ponder His foretaste of the cup*
> *Then to the cross repair*

and we will do so using six pointers:- 1. The Passage; 2. The Place; 3. The Parable; 4. The Peril; 5. The Person and His Prayer ,and 6. The Prospect.

1. The Passage

As with other important milestones in the earthly life of Christ, the Holy Spirit has recorded the account of Gethsemane for us no less than three times in Holy Scripture – see Matthew 26:36-46; Mark 14:32-42 and Luke 22:39-46. There is also a possible allusion to the event in Hebrews 5:7 where we read *In the days of His flesh, Jesus offered up prayers and supplications, with loud cries and tears, to Him who was able to save Him from death, and He was heard for His godly fear.*

I said that Gethsemene is familiar soil. It is, but this should not detract from the fact that it is also exceedingly holy ground. Here in Gethsemene we are allowed the privilege of looking in on an intimate communion between God the Father and God the Son. Perhaps we too should be on our knees when we read this sacred portion. Only Peter, James and John - the inner three of the twelve disciples - were allowed to witness such an intimate occasion – just as they were the only disciples allowed to be present at the raising of Jairus's daughter and the Transfiguration.

2. The Place

A place which was called Gethsemane

It would seem that this garden was one of Jesus's favourite haunts. John relates that *Jesus often met there with His disciples*

(John 18:2). Come with me in your mind's eye to modern day Jerusalem. Go to the east of the city and cross over the Kidron valley. Now you are at the Mount of Olives, with its olive tree covered slopes. Ascending a little way you will come to a grotto or a garden - the garden of Gethsemane!

The name 'Kidron' means 'dark, murky' which is very significant considering what was going on at this milestone in Jesus's life. The name 'Gethsemane' means 'olive press' which, as we shall shortly see, is also most significant. Even today there are olive trees in Gethsemane. The olive tree is of the kind that always renews itself, and some of the trees in Gethsemane are believed to be two thousand years old. One does not have to look closely at their trunks to see that they are very twisted and gnarled, as though they are writhing in agony. Did these trees really see the Lord of Glory prostrate in agonised prayer? If only they could talk.

History began in a garden. Genesis 2:8 reads *The Lord God planted a garden in Eden, in the east; and there He put the man whom He had formed.* History - for the redeemed - will end in a garden, the garden city of the New Jerusalem. Revelation 22: 1 ff describes *the river of the water of life bright as crystal, flowing . . . through the middle of the street of the city; also, on either side of the river, the tree of life with its twelve kinds of fruit, yielding its fruit each month; and the leaves of the tree were for the healing of the nations. There shall no more be anything accursed . . .* History was transformed by two gardens: 1. The Garden of Gethsemane and 2. *Now in the place where He was crucified there was a garden, and in the garden a new tomb where no one had ever been laid* (John 19:41). We are here considering the former garden: Gethsemane, the garden of the olive press.

3. The Parable

Gethsemane, 'the olive press'. Olive trees and olive oil were central to the economy of Israel in biblical days – just as coal used to be integral to the economy of South Wales, from where I write these lines. The olive tree symbolised the land of Israel. Deuteronomy 8: 7,8 describes Canaan as *a good land . . . a land of olive trees.* Follow closely the 'Parable of the Olive Tree'.

The Production. One olive tree contained approximately ten to fifteen gallons of olive oil. It was produced as follows: First of all the tree was beaten with rods so that the olives fell off. These olives were then gathered and put into a large, circular mill made of stone. A top stone was then harnessed to an animal, who was blindfolded, and made to walk in circles. In walking,so the olives were crushed and their oil oozed out. The oil was then tapped into jars as it ran through holes drilled into the stone. This was the best oil, but the process was not over. In the mill much pulp was left which was then taken and put into a wooden olive press, to extract the very last drop of olive oil. The oil from this wooden mill though was the poorer oil, used primarily for lighting lamps. So the whole process was rather long and slow, and involved the bruising of the olives - yet a happy result ensued:-

The Produce. The resultant olive oil was most desirable:-

It was **food** - a staple part of the diet in those days.

Olive oil also meant **light,** as it was burned in the lamps for fuel. When we recall the fear of darkness in biblical times - days before the discovery of electricity and neon - we glean something of the vitality of olive oil.

Olive oil also meant **medicine** - *Thou anointest my head with oil* (Psalm 23:5), *he . . . bound up his wounds, pouring on oil* (Luke 10:34).

The Picture. The production of olive oil mirrors the experience of none less than the Lord Jesus Christ. First of all He was beaten - beaten by both the religious and political authorities. Then following on from His beating He was put into the 'olive press'. Isaiah 53:5 relates prophetically He was *wounded for our transgressions, He was bruised for our iniquities; upon Him was the chastisement that made us whole, and with His stripes we are healed.* The result of this painful olive press though is infinitely good and desirable:-

Jesus is our **food.** He said *I am the bread of life. He who comes to me shall not hunger and he who believes in me shall never thirst* (John 6:35).

Jesus is also our **light.** He said *I am the light of the world. He who follows me will not walk in darkness but will have the light of life* (John 8:12).

Jesus is also our **medicine.** He heals our deepest, direst ailment, for His death on the cross for our sins heals our broken relationship with God. Jesus said *Those who are well have no need of a physician, but those who are sick; I came not to call the righteous, but sinners* (Mark 2:17).

The Paraclete. Oil, in the Bible is often used to symbolise the Holy Spirit. A further result of the 'Calvary olive press' was the pouring out of the Holy Spirit on the earth. *As yet the Spirit had not been given, because Jesus was not yet glorified* (John 7:39). It is the Holy Spirit who applies the work of Calvary to our souls, and makes it effective. 'We are made partakers of the redemption purchased by Christ by the effectual application of it to us by His Holy Spirit' (*Shorter Catechism,* Q. 29).

4. The Peril

It is evident from Gethsemane that there was something about Jesus's impending death which caused Him to shudder to the very core of His being. What a contrast this was, a sceptic might object, with, for example, the Protestant Martyrs who faced being burned at stake with great fortitude, courage and even cheer. Verse 33 of our account though tells us that as Jesus contemplated Calvary He *began to be greatly distressed and troubled.* We may wonder why this was, and the answer is given in verse 36. Jesus shuddered at *the cup* which He was about to drink, and even asked that the Father would remove it from Him if it was His will. The peril therefore refers to the cup - the cup of suffering.

In the Bible 'the cup' can be either a blessing or a bane; a cup of joy or a cup of judgment. In this case the cup refers most definitely to the latter. It refers no less to the awful and indescribable cup of the wrath of God. Other Scriptures illustrate this for us:- *In the hand of the Lord there is a cup, with foaming wine, well mixed; and He will pour a draft from it, and all the wicked of the earth shall drain it down to the dregs* (Psalm 75:8). . . . *you who have drunk at the hand of the Lord the cup of His wrath, who have drunk to the dregs the bowl of staggering* (Isaiah 51:17). *God remembered great Babylon, to make her drain the cup of the fury of His wrath* (Revelation 16:9).

Jesus shrank then, not so much from His impending physical sufferings (agonising though they were to be) but rather from the *spiritual* sufferings He was to about to undergo on the sinner's behalf. It is beyond human imagining to ever realise what it must have been like for the sinless One to be made sin. *For our sake He made Him to be sin who knew no sin, so that in Him we might become the righteousness of God* (2 Corinthians 5:21). It is beyond our comprehesion to imagine what it would be like for One Person to bear the sins of all God's elect in a moment of time, along with God's holy wrath and righteous indignation upon them. *The wages of sin is death* (Romans 6:23), and Jesus sweat drops of blood at the contemplation of suffering such a spiritual death. 1 Peter 2:24 tells us *He Himself bore our sins in His body on the tree.* If we know our own hearts we will tremble at the thought of His bearing God's wrath just upon our own sins, let alone upon the sins of all God's people.

The time when Jesus was literally 'God forsaken' at Calvary, when He stood in the sinners stead, was literally the most terrible time of all history. What a cup it was, incomparable and insurpassable. Yet paradoxically, the time was also the most wonderful time of all history, for His cup of suffering is our cup of salvation. The Psalmist wrote *What shall I render to the Lord for all His bounty to me? I will lift up the cup of salvation and call on the name of the Lord* (Psalm 116:12,13). We may state reverently that in drinking the cup, Jesus drank damnation dry. With one dire draught, my divine deliverer drank damnation dry for me! Thank God that Jesus faced the peril. In doing so He has delivered us from it.

> *Death and the curse were in our cup*
> *O Christ 'twas full for Thee*
> *But Thou hast drained the last dark drop*
> *'Tis empty now for me*
> *That bitter cup, love drank it up*
> *Now blessing's draught for me*

5. The Person and His Prayer

Gethsemane reveals Jesus to be both i. The Sympathetic Man and ii. The Second Man

i. The Sympathetic Man

Jesus knows your sorrow, Jesus knows your care. Gethsemane shows very graphically that Jesus knows what it is like to suffer. Our God is human too! *We have not a high priest who is unable to sympathise with our weaknesses* (Hebrews 4:14).

ii. The Second Man

What a contrast there is between Eden and Gethsemane, between the first and second Adams. The first Adam brought destruction to all his descendants because He rebelled against the will of God. The second Adam brings deliverance to all His descendants because He submitted to the will of God. Eden was characterised by assertion against the will of God. It resulted in sweat, thorns, the curse of God and separation from God for all of the first Adam's descendants. Gethsemane was characterised by acceptance of the will of God. It too led to sweat (see Luke 22:44), thorns (a crown of thorns) and being cursed by God. But happily, Gethsemane results ultimately in reconciliation to God for all of the Second Adam's descendants. Eden was a garden of death. Gethsemane was a garden of life. The heart of the matter is seen in Jesus's prayer: *Not what I will but what Thou wilt.*

> *For me it was in the garden*
> *He prayed 'Not my will but Thine'*
> *He had no tears for His own griefs*
> *But sweat drops of blood for mine*

Whilst Adam, in Eden, was disobedient. Jesus, the Second Adam, in Gethsemane was obedient. *He became obedient unto death, even death on a cross* (Philippians 2:8). He prayed *My Father, if this cannot pass unless I drink it, THY WILL BE DONE* (Matthew 26:42). Romans 5:18,19 brings out the contrast between the two Adam's most succinctly:- *As one man's trespass led to condemnation for all men, so one man's act of righteousness leads to acquittal and life for all men. For as by one man's disobedience many were made sinners, so by one man's obedience many will be made righteous.* Finally, we consider

6. The Prospect

In Gethsemane, as Jesus awaited His arrest, He prayed. The prospect of Calvary and all that it was to mean lay right in front of Him.

The worst conceivable prospect that could happen to God's Christ would be to be betrayed by a friend, denied by a friend, forsaken by His friends, unjustly tried, cruelly treated, humiliated, nailed to a cross and hung up naked to die on a public thoroughfare as people walked by laughing. Worst of all would be to be forsaken by God the Father as He bore the sins of all God's people in a moment of time. This worst, horror of horrors, actually happened to Him.

The worst conceivable prospect that could happen to God's child would be . . . illness, injury, mental breakdown, redundancy, loneliness, bereavement, poverty, failure . . . ? No. The worst that could happen to anyone would be to be separated from God in hell - separated from the source of all life, light and love. The worst happened to Christ, but on the authority of the Bible we may be assured that the worst will never happen to us! The worst will never happen to us because the worst happened to Him! Jesus was separated from God in time so that we might be reconciled to God for all eternity. Romans 8 begins *There is therefore now no condemnation for those who are in Christ Jesus.* Romans 8 ends explaining that absolutely nothing *can separate us from the love of God in Christ Jesus our Lord.*

Gethsemane led to Gabbath. Gabbath led to Golgotha. At Golgotha salvation was wrought. Golgotha led to Glory for Jesus, and will lead to Glory for all who trust in Him.

> *Lest I forget Gethsemane*
> *Lest I forget Thine agony*
> *Lest I forget Thy love for me*
> *Lead me to Calvary*

CHAPTER NINE

The Milestone Of His Cross

Now at the feast he used to release for them one prisoner for whom they asked. And among the rebels in prison, who had committed murder in the insurrection, there was a man called Barabbas. And the crowd came up and began to ask Pilate to do as he was wont to do for them. And he answered them, 'Do you want me to release for you the King of the Jews?' For he perceived that it was out of envy that the chief priests had delivered Him up. But the chief priests stirred up the crowd to have him release for them Barabbas instead. And Pilate again said to them, 'Then what shall I do with the Man Whom you call the King of the Jews?' And they cried out again, 'Crucify Him.' And Pilate said to them, 'Why, what evil has He done?' But they shouted all the more, 'Crucify Him.' So Pilate, wishing to satisfy the crowd, released for them Barabbas; and having scourged Jesus, he delivered Him to be crucified.

And the soldiers led Him away inside the palace (that is, the praetorium); and they called together the whole battalion. And they clothed Him in a purple cloak, and plaiting a crown of thorns they put it on Him. And they began to salute Him, 'Hail, King of the Jews!' And they struck His head with a reed, and spat upon Him, and they knelt down in homage to Him. And when they had mocked Him, they stripped Him of the purple cloak, and put His Own clothes on Him. And they led Him out to crucify Him.

And they compelled a passer-by, Simon of Cyrene, who was coming in from the country, the father of Alexander and Rufus, to carry His cross. And they brought Him to the place called Golgotha (which means the place of a skull). And they offered Him wine mingled with myrrh; but He did not take it. And they crucified Him, and divided His garments among them, casting lots for them, to decide what each should take. And it was the third hour, when they crucified Him. And the inscription of the charge against Him read, 'The King of the

Jews.' And with Him they crucified two robbers, one on His right and one on His left. And those who passed by derided Him, wagging their heads, and saying, 'Aha! You Who would destroy the temple and build it in three days, save Yourself and come down from the cross!' So also the chief priests mocked Him to one another with the scribes, saying, 'He saved others; He cannot save Himself. Let the Christ, the King of Israel, come down now from the cross, that we may see and believe.' Those who were crucified with Him also reviled Him.

And when the sixth hour had come, there was darkness over the whole land until the ninth hour. And at the ninth hour Jesus cried with a loud voice, 'Eloi, Eloi, lama sabachthani?' which means, 'My God, My God, why hast Thou forsaken Me?' And some of the bystanders hearing it said, 'Behold, He is calling Elijah.' And one ran and, filling a sponge full of vinegar, put it on a reed and gave it to Him to drink, saying, 'Wait, let us see whether Elijah will come to take Him down.' And Jesus uttered a loud cry and breathed His last. And the curtain of the temple was torn in two, from top to bottom. And when the centurion, who stood facing Him, saw that He thus breathed His last, he said, 'Truly, this Man was the Son of God!' (Mark 15:6-39).

The death of Jesus on the Cross for our sins was more than a major milestone in the life of Christ. Calvary is the heart of the heart, and the centre of the centre of biblical Christianity.

The four Gospels have been described as 'four Passion narratives with extended introductions' and the description is a good one. It is a fact that the Bible devotes more space to the six hours when Jesus hung on the cross than to anything else. Jesus was born to die. The earliest Christian creed teaches with precision *that Christ died for our sins in accordance with the Scriptures* (1 Corinthians 15:3). The later so-called 'Apostles Creed' goes straight from Jesus being 'born of the Virgin Mary' to the fact that

He 'suffered under Pontius Pilate, and was crucified, dead and buried.'

Christianity is 'cross-tianity.' The Old Testament anticipates, prophecies and prefigures the death of Christ. The Gospels describe to us the death of Christ in fulfilment of the Old Testament. The epistles of the New Testament explain and apply the death of Christ. The believer trusts in the death of Christ for full salvation. The Church's main message is *Jesus Christ and Him crucified* (1 Corinthians 2:2) and when believers meet to gather around the Lord's Table, the bread and wine of which they partake symbolises none other but the broken body and shed blood of their living Saviour, as the communion recalls and remembers the death of Christ on Calvary's cross. And if this is not enough, even heaven itself sings and celebrates the death of Christ. The chorus of heaven is joyfully clear: *Worthy is the Lamb who was slain* (Revelation 5:12).

Calvary is all about the redeeming blood and dying love of the Lord Jesus Christ. We cannot think about the cross too much or ever begin to exhaust its contents. It will take us an eternity to fathom the love of God in Christ on the cross. It is the theme of a million hymns. In speaking of the cross of course, we refer to the work of the cross as opposed to the wood of the cross. The emblem worn around the necks of many is powerless to save. Yet the expiation wrought on the old rugged cross, outside the walls of Jerusalem two thousand years ago is still the power of God for salvation to every one who has faith. Our focus therefore should be not so much on the crucifixion but on the Crucified. With Pilgrim we would sing:-

> *Blest cross! Blest sepulchre! Blest rather be*
> *The Man that there was put to death for me.*

Of the many angles of approach we could take, let us consider the milestone of the cross from five perspectives:-

1. The Two Characters
2. The Timeless Cross
3. The Tumultuous Catastrophe and the Terrible Cry
4. The Torn Curtain
5. The Telling Confession of the Testifying Centurion

1. The Two Characters

Of the many 'dramatis personae' in Mark's account of the crucifixion, we will here consider just two, namely Barabbas and Simon of Cyrene. With a little attention we can see ourselves mirrored in these two men. Both give us some insight into what it means to be a Christian:-

i. Barabbas

... among the rebels in prison, who had committed murder ... was a man called Barabbas ... Pilate ... released for them Barabbas; and having scourged Jesus, He delivered Him to be crucified .

Let us place ourselves in Barabbas's shoes: a criminal, caught, tried, found guilty, condemned to death, in prison awaiting the death penalty - and then FREED! What a joyful release it must have been for Barabbas - and yet he was not released automatically, but at Someone Else's expense. Barabbas was freed only because Another One went to die in his place.

Every Christian can relate to Barabbas. We are all sinners by nature as well as by practice. We are all condemned and awaiting God's judgment - but we can all go free because of Jesus! He died in our place. He suffered God's wrath to deliver us from it. Jesus actually tasted the full brunt of spiritual death to give us life. The Bible affirms in crystal clear terms:- *There is therefore now no condemnation for those who are in Christ Jesus. For the law of the Spirit of life in Christ Jesus has set me free from the law of sin and death* (Romans 8:1,2).

We can all relate to Barabbas. He was a guilty sinner and yet a saved sinner - saved by the death of Jesus in his room and stead.

ii. Simon of Cyrene

Cyrene is modern day Libya. *They compelled a passer-by, Simon of Cyrene, who was coming in from the country, the father of Alexander and Rufus, to carry His cross ...* (15:21).

In Romans 16:13, Paul writes *Greet Rufus, eminent in the Lord.* If this was the same Rufus, Simon of Cyrene's son (and Mark like Paul was also writing to those in Rome) then Rufus's father became a saved man, and handed on his precious faith to at least one of his sons.

Simon of Cyrene appears here, and here alone in the sacred volume. He comes on and off the scene for just the one purpose for which he is so famous: he carried the cross of the Lord Jesus Christ. Every Christian is a Barabbas, but every Christian is a Simon too. Jesus said *If any man would come after Me, let him deny himself and take up his cross and follow Me* (Mark 8:34). But what exactly does it mean to 'take up the cross'?:-

i.   It means being identified with Jesus in a faith-union. Paul wrote *If we have been united with Him in a death like His, we shall certainly be united with Him in a resurrection like His* (Romans 6:5).

ii. It means an end to all worldly/earthly hopes and an awareness that the world to come is impending. Carrying our cross means that our hope is not in ourselves or in this world, but rather, just like Abraham who *looked forward to the city which has foundations, whose builder and maker is God* (Hebrews 11:10).

iii. Carrying our cross speaks of the scorn of the world. Christianity will never be popular. Our Saviour was *despised and rejected by men* (Isaiah 53:3). We who follow Him can expect nothing less. We too are to take up the cross. It is encapsulated in Hebrews 13:13,14:- *Therefore let us go forth to Him outside the camp, and bear the abuse He endured. For here we have no lasting city, but we seek the city which is to come.*

Take up thy cross the Saviour said
if thou wouldst My disciple be
Deny thyself, the world forsake
and humbly follow after Me

Take up thy cross, nor heed the shame
Nor let thy foolish pride rebel
Thy Lord for thee the cross endured
To save thy soul from death and hell

Barabbas and Simon of Cyrene. They are two characters of many, and yet they are typical characters. Both of them seem to mirror ourselves and our relationship to the crucified Saviour.

2. The Timeless Cross

And they brought Him to the place called Golgotha (which means the place of the skull) ... And they crucified Him . . .

Mark is very economical with his words as he tells us of the Event of events. In considering this, the timeless cross, we come to the heart of the Christian Faith. We now move from the holy place and step into the Holy of holies.

Sweet the moments, rich in blessing
Which before the cross I spend
Life and health and peace possessing
from the sinner's dying Friend

Here I rest, for ever viewing
mercy poured in streams of blood
Precious drops, my soul bedewing
Plead and claim my peace with God.

The timeless cross of Christ - towering o'er the wrecks of time. Note that it was:- according to Scripture and ii. an atoning sacrifice.

i. It was according to Scripture

When Christ died, the soldiers *divided His garments among them, casting lots for them, to decide what each should take* (15:24). Exactly a thousand years earlier, David penned these eery lines in Psalm 22:16-18:- *they have pierced My hands and My feet - I can count all My bones - they stare and gloat over Me; they divide My garments among them and for My rainment they cast lots.* We read too that *those who passed by derided Him, wagging their heads...* (15:29). In the same Psalm 22, in verses 7 and 8, David captured this also:- *All who see Me mock at Me, they make mouths at Me, they wag their heads; He committed His cause to the Lord, let Him deliver Him, let Him rescue Him, for He delights in Him.* All this being so, we can only confess in total agreement with that early Christian confession of faith, that *Christ died for our sins in accordance with the Scriptures* (1 Corinthians 15:3).

ii. It was an atoning sacrifice

What evil has He done? (15:14) asked Pilate. The implicit answer is a resounding 'None!' Jesus had no sins of His own for which He deserved punishment. He died, not for His own sins, for He had none. He died for the sins of others. *He was wounded for our transgressions* (Isaiah 53:5), *Who was put to death for our trespasses* (Romans 4:25).

A holy God must punish sin, or He would cease to be God. In Christ, God both punished sin and pardoned the sinner - *sending*

His Own Son in the likeness of sinful flesh and for sin, He con-
demned sin in the flesh in order that the just requirement of the
law might be fulfilled in us (Romans 8:3,4). What a God! He
provided a salvation for His people which did full justice to both
His holiness and His love. *It was to prove at the present time that*
He Himself is righteous and that He justifies him who has faith in
Jesus (Romans 3:26). *God shows His love for us in that while we*
were yet sinners Christ died for us (Romans 5:8).

And so we can see that the timeless cross was both i. according
to Scripture and ii. atoning for sin.

> *Guilty, vile and helpless we*
> *Spotless Lamb of God was He*
> *Full atonement - can it be?*
> *Hallelujah! What a Saviour!*

3.   The Tumultuous Catastrophe and the Terrible Cry

Of the many literally awe-full and earth shattering events that
happened at Calvary, arguably the most graphic was:- *when the*
sixth hour had come there was darkness over the whole land until
the ninth hour. And at the ninth hour Jesus cried with a loud voice
'Eloi, Eloi, lama sabachthani?' which means 'My God, My God,
why hast Thou forsaken Me?' (15:33). These are awesome lines.
We must tread very carefully, cautiously and reverently. Consider
though:- i. the darkness and ii. the dereliction.

i.   The darkness

Darkness at midday! Darkness often refers to Divine judgment
in the Bible:- *... on that day, says the Lord, I will make the sun go*
down at noon, and darken the earth in broad daylight (Amos
8:9). *The sun shall be turned into darkness* (Joel 2:31). Likewise,
one of the judgments upon an unrepentant Pharaoh in Egypt was
thick darkness in all the land of Egypt (for) three days (Exodus

10:22). So we can state loudly and clearly that on the cross Jesus did indeed suffer the darkness of God's judgment upon our sins, to save our souls.

Well might the sun in darkness hide
And shut his glories in
When Christ the mighty Maker died
For man the creature's sin

ii. The dereliction

My God, My God, why hast Thou forssaken Me?

Hell is eternal separation from the love of God and the God of love. Hell is spiritual death. It is the worst that could possibly happen to anyone. So bad is it, that Jesus had to die a death like this to save us from it. The torments of His soul dwarfed even the excrutiating physical pains of His body. Jesus died spiritually as well as physically. God, according to Habakkuk 1:12 is *of purer eyes than to behold evil and canst not look on wrong.* On the cross, Paul tells us, *For our sake He made Him to be sin Who knew no sin* (2 Corinthians 5:21).

Christ took our sins at Calvary. God therefore turned away from Him. It is awful - and yet it is wonderful. His alienation is our reconciliation. His hell is our heaven. His judgment is our justification. His agony is our atonement. His dereliction - the worst that could happen to Him - will result in our eternal delight. *He shall see the fruit of the travail of His soul and be satisfied* (Isaiah 53:11). Because of both the darkness and dereliction our Divine deliverer underwent on our behalf, we may be certain that absolutely nothing, in time or eternity *will be able to separate us from the love of God in Christ Jesus our Lord* (Romans 8:39).

The tumultuous catastrophe (the darkness) and the terrible cry (the dereliction). In a sense, they are beyond human explanation, and yet they give us heart when we find ourselves in the darker moments of our human experience:-

Lord, should fear and anguish roll
Darkly o'er my sinful soul
Thou, Who once was thus bereft
That Thine Own might ne'er be left
Teach me by that bitter cry
In the gloom to know Thee nigh

4. The Torn Curtain

Another miracle that occurred at Calvary. Again, it is beyond human explanation, for no mere human reason can explain how *the curtain of the temple was torn in two, from top to bottom* (Mark 15:38).

The tearing of the temple curtain made such an impact that all three synoptic Gospels record it. The temple was so historic and meaningful, that such an event was momentous. In Acts 6:7 we read *a great many of the priests were obedient to the faith.* It may well be that this event had something to do with it.

i. The background

The temple veil was the curtain hanging between the holy place and the holy of holies. God dwelt in the holy of holies in a very special and particular way. All were barred from entering and approaching this most holiest of places - all except the high priest, and he only once a year on the day of atonement. The temple curtain thus speaks of the separation of sinful humanity from a thrice-holy God.

ii. The blessing

Jesus's death ripped up the temple veil! He takes away the barrier of sin. Hebrews 10:19 ff assures us:- *we have confidence to enter the sanctuary by the blood of Jesus, by the new and living way which He opened up for us through the curtain, that is, through*

His flesh. Similarly, in Ephesians 2:18:- *through Him we both have access in one Spirit to the Father* - the rent veil being tangible evidence that this is indeed so. For our final point in our study of Mark's account of the milestone of the cross, let us consider:-

5. The Telling Confession of the Testifying Centurion

Writing to his friends in Rome, Mark chose to tell them about the Roman Centurion present supervising the crucifixion at Calvary. This man had no doubt supervised many such gory killings before - it was his job. But he knew that there was something drastically different about this One:- *And when the centurion, who stood facing Him, saw that He thus breathed His last, he said 'Truly this Man was the Son of God.'* (15:39). Here then, at the close of Mark's Gospel, we see a heathen man drawn to Christ and lead to confess His name.

Jesus is indeed the Son of God and God the Son. Mark began his Gospel:- *The Gospel of Jesus Christ, the Son of God* (Mark 1:1). He draws it to a close here with *Truly, this Man was the Son of God.* Mark records the Gerasene demoniac's shouting *Jesus, Son of the most high God* (Mark 5:7). We saw at Jesus's baptism how a voice came from heaven *Thou art My beloved Son, with Thee I am well pleased* (Mark 1:11). Likewise, on the Mount of Transfiguration, we heard the testimony of heaven:- *This is My beloved Son, listen to Him* (Mark 9:7).

It is because He is Who He is, that Jesus can do what He does. His worth affects His work and His character affects His cross. It is because Jesus was and is the eternal Son of God that He was able to give His life as a ransom for many (cf Mark 10:45). On the cross, Christ paid the ransom price for our sins once and for all. Jesus's death on the cross frees us from the slavery of sin, and gives us the desire to be the slaves of God. If we are His, we can be most certain that we are saved for time and eternity, and there is no freedom comparable with being in bondage to God!

Lord of the cross of shame
Set my cold heart aflame
With love for You, my Saviour and my Master
Who on that lonely day
Bore all my sins away
And saved me from the judgment and disaster.

CHAPTER TEN

The Milestone Of His Resurrection

He was raised on the third day in accordance with the Scriptures
(1 Corinthians 15:3).

Remember Jesus Christ, risen from the dead . . .
(2 Timothy 2:8).

Christ's resurrection from the grave was more than a milestone at the end of a most unusual earthly life. It is in fact the shorthand for the whole Christian Faith. So integral to Christianity is the resurrection of Christ that Paul could state *if Christ has not been raised then our preaching is in vain and your faith is in vain . . . If Christ has not been raised, your faith is futile and you are still in your sins* (1 Corinthians 15:14,17).

Christianity proclaims a risen Saviour, that is, the Jesus who was laid to rest in Joseph of Arimathea's tomb, having died on the cross for our sins, overcame death by rising again three days later in the same body in which He had been buried. The resurrection is the distinguishing mark of the Christian Faith, and on it the whole Faith stands or falls. The resurrection of Christ is so central to the New Testament that if we open its pages anywhere, we will find Christ's resurrection somewhere, implicitly or explicitly. The first Christian sermon ever recorded proclaims of Jesus *God raised Him up, having loosed the pangs of death, because it was not possible for Him to be held by it . . . He was not abandoned to hades, nor did His flesh see corruption. This Jesus God raised up, and of that we are all witnesses* (Acts 2:24,31,32). Then in the very last book of the inspired volume, we hear the risen Christ say *I am the first and the last and the living one, I died, and behold I am alive for evermore, and I have the keys of death and hades* (Revelation 1:18,19).

1. The Plain Resurrection Fact

The resurrection of Christ has been called 'the most attested fact in history.' An impartial study of the New Testament reveals three stubborn facts - facts highly embarrassing and awkward to unbelievers. The facts are i. Christ's tomb was empty, ii. The risen Christ appeared and was seen by many, iii. Certain effects are inexplicable unless they have Christ's resurrection as their cause.

i. The Vacated Sepulchre

He is not here; for He has risen as He said. Come see the place where He lay (Matthew 28:6) said the angel to some women – women who certainly were not expecting such an occurrence. The fact that women are recorded as being the first witnesses of Christ's empty tomb is striking. In the ancient world, the status of women was such that they were disqualified from giving evidence in court. Surely then, if the account of this incident is a product of creative writing, Matthew would have at least ensured that men - and men of some stature - would have been the first witnesses of the empty tomb.

John's Gospel records the first wary visit of Peter and John to Christ's empty tomb. As a Gospel writer, John is honest and candid, and relates that, contrary to both the Old Testament and Christ's own many predictions, he and Peter did not expect a resurrection - *for as yet they did not know the Scripture, that He must rise from the dead* (John 20:9). The vivid eye-witness details however prove that in dealing with the empty tomb we are dealing in fact not fiction. Peter *went into the tomb; he saw the linen cloths lying;*

and the napkin, which had been on His head, not lying with the linen cloths but rolled up in a place by itself (John 20:6,7).

ii. The Victorious Saviour

We have five different, independent accounts of the risen Christ's resurrection appearances – Matthew, Mark, Luke, John and Paul. This, on the Bible's own criteria, is more than enough to substantiate the truth of the case, for *A single witness shall not prevail . . . only on the evidence of two witnesses, or of three witnesses, shall a charge be sustained* (Deuteronomy 19:15). In relating the risen Christ's appearances, each Gospel writer tells the same basic story, yet differs in minor details from the others. This gives the lie to any thought of collusion between the four Gospel reporters. It is similar in a human court of law today. Evidence concerning the same event is sure to differ in detail, depending on the witnesses' angle and vantage point. The differences however do not mean that the event never happened at all. True evidence entails that there is no collusion, concoction or collision between the various witnesses. The evidence for Christ's resurrection is such. Let us then catalogue the vast amount of evidence for the risen Christ's resurrection appearances:-

Matthew records that Christ appeared to:-
1. Mary Magdalene and the other Mary (28:9 ff)
2. The eleven disciples on a mountain in Galilee (28:16 ff)

Mark records that Christ appeared to:-
1. Mary Magdalene (16:9)
2. Two disciples as they were walking into the country (16:12)
3. The eleven disciples at table (16:14 ff)

Luke records that Christ appeared to:-
1. Two disciples on the road to Emmaus (24:13 ff)
2. Simon Peter (24:34)

3. The eleven disciples (24:36)

John records that Christ appeared to:-
1. Mary Magdalene (20:11)
2. The disciples minus Thomas (20:19 ff)
3. The disciples with Thomas (20:26)
4. Seven disciples by the Sea of Galilee (21:1 ff)

Then **Paul**, in 1 Corinthians 15 - evidence which predates even the Gospels - records how Christ appeared to:-
1. Peter
2. The twelve
3. A group of more than five hundred people at once, most of whom were still around to substantiate the fact
4. James (the Lord's initially unbelieving brother, see John 7:5)
5. All the apostles
6. Paul himself, whilst he was vehemently opposed to Christianity in every shape and form.

The cumulative evidence for the risen Christ's appearances therefore makes the fact irrefutable. The fact of the resurrection has never been explained away. *He presented Himself alive after His passion by many proofs, appearing to them during forty days* (Acts 1:3).

iii. The Verifying Signs

If every cause has an effect or catalyst, even more evidence for Christ's resurrection accumulates. Christ's resurrection accounts for, amongst other things:-

1. The total transformation of His disciples from frightened hide-aways to bold preachers of the resurrection of Christ. Compare John 20:19 with Acts 4:13 and 33: *The doors being shut where the disciples were, for fear of the Jews* (John 20:19) with *Now*

when they saw the boldness of Peter and John . . . And with great power the apostles gave their testimony to the resurrection of the Lord Jesus (Acts 4:13,33). All bar one of the eleven disciples died a violent death for his belief in Christ's resurrection. The one exception was John, who was exiled for his faith. Such tenacity would not have been shown if they knew in their heart of hearts that Christ did not actually rise from the dead.

2. How do we account for the change of the Sabbath from the seventh day (Saturday) to the first day (Sunday, known now as the Lord's Day) if Christ did not conquer the grave on that particular day? The early disciples were all Jews, and the Saturday Sabbath was a custom of antiquity, hallowed and inviolable. Old traditions die hard. Yet after Christ's resurrection they exchanged the seventh day for the first day, as the day on which to meet together to worship the risen Christ.

3. How do we account for the growth of the Christian Church for the last two thousand years since the apostle's time if the resurrection is untrue? The Church did not create Christ's resurrection, rather, Christ's resurrection created the Church.

4. How do we account for the individual Christian experience of salvation if Christ is dead? Are the millions of Christians worldwide, from all strata of society, all deluded? It cannot be so. Personal testimony sings:-

> *I serve a risen Saviour, He's in the world today*
> *I know that He is living, whatever men may say*
> *I see His hand of mercy, I hear His voice of cheer*
> *And just the time I need Him He's always near*
>
> *He lives! He lives! Christ Jesus lives today!*
> *He walks with me and talks with me, along life's narrow way*
> *He lives! He lives! salvation to impart*
> *You ask me how I know He lives? He lives within my heart!*

2. The Precious Resurrection Faith

Having considered the irrefutable fact of Christ's resurrection, we come now to consider its meaning. The New Testament teaches that Christ's resurrection has at least three implications for the Christian Faith. The resurrection, the Bible explains is; i. The Proof of the Saviour's Godhood, ii. The Pardon of the Sinner's Guilt, iii. The Pledge of the Saved's Glory.

i. The Proof of the Saviour's Godhood

Christ's resurrection is the final and key proof of His deity. The resurrection proves that the One Who arose from the grave on the third day is none other than God Himself. Paul proclaimed that Jesus Christ was *designated Son of God in power by the Spirit of holiness by His resurrection from the dead* (Romans 1:3). The resurrection is the Miracle of miracles, but in perfect accord with the rest of Christ's life: the virgin womb corroborates the virgin tomb; His raising of others corroborates His own rising; His sinless life logically entails His exemption from the law of sin, death and corruption, and His saving, vicarious death is the other side of the coin to His superlative, victorious resurrection.

Jesus once made this staggering claim about Himself: *I am the resurrection and the life; he who believes in me, though he die, yet shall he live, and whoever lives and believes in me shall never die* (John 11:25,26). His own resurrection proves that He was speaking the sane and sober truth.

Jesus assures all God's elect *this is the will of Him who sent me, that I should lose nothing of all that He has given me, but raise it up at the last day* (John 6:38) and *No one can come to me unless the Father who sent me draws him; and I will raise him up at the last day* (John 6:44). His own resurrection confirms and authenticates His claims.

Jesus actually prophesied that He would rise from the grave on the third day. *And He began to teach them that the Son of Man must suffer many things . . . and be killed, and after three days rise again. And He said this plainly* (see Mark 8:31, 9:31 and 10:33). Then in John 10:17,18 we read Him saying *I lay down my life that I may take it again. No one takes it from me, but I lay it down of my own accord. I have power to lay it down, and I have power to take it again . . .* In saying such things, was He deluded or Divine? A trickster or the Truth? An imposter or Immanuel? A liar, lunatic or Lord? His resurrection proves that the latter is true in each case. *God raised Him from the dead* (Acts 13:30). *He has risen, AS HE SAID* (Matthew 28:6). It all proves His total and absolute deity. Jesus Christ is God! *designated Son of God in power . . . by His resurrection from the dead* (Romans 1:4).

ii. The Pardon of the Sinner's Guilt

The Christian's eternal salvation is based on Christ's resurrection. Our new life is a result of His resurrected life. Peter exclaimed:- *Blessed be the God and Father of our Lord Jesus Christ! By His great mercy we have been born anew to a living hope through the resurrection of Jesus Christ from the dead* (1 Peter 1:3). Paul proclaimed (probably quoting an early Christian creed) *if you confess with your lips that Jesus is Lord and believe in your heart that God raised Him from the dead you will be saved* (Romans 10:9). On this verse Geoffrey Wilson makes the comment 'The part is put for the whole, for to believe that 'God has raised Christ from the dead, involves the belief that Christ is all that He claimed to be, and that He has accomplished all that He came to perform' (Hodge)' John Calvin explains:-

> 'Our salvation is thus divided between the death and resurrection of Christ . . . We must remember that when in Scripture Christ's death alone is mentioned, everything to do with His resurrection is included. In the same way, when the resurrection alone is mentioned, everything to do with Christ's death is included . . . He obtained the victory by

rising again and became the resurrection and the life . . .' (*Institutes* II,16,13).

In what could be described as a 'nutshell verse,' Paul states in Romans 4:25 that Christ *was put to death for our trespasses and raised for our justification.* The resurrection can be considered as the divine seal of approval of God the Father upon His Son's atoning sacrifice for sinners on Calvary's cross. On Calvary Christ paid the debt we owe to God the Father because of our sin (see Colossians 2:14). God the Father accepted His payment, and gave His 'received with thanks' – His divine receipt being His raising Christ from the dead. The death and resurrection of Christ then are the two sides of the one salvation coin. R. A. Torrey expands:-

> 'Christ gave His life a propitiation for believers. He was delivered up for our transgressions. The Resurrection settles it beyond peradventure that God accepted the propitiation. The resurrection is God's declaration of His acceptance of the propitiation and is, therefore, the declaration of our justification . . . By the resurrection, God declares that He has accepted and is satisfied with the settlement Christ has made. I am declared righteous in His sight. If we are ever troubled with doubts as to whether God has accepted the offering Christ made, we have only to look at the empty tomb of the Risen Lord.'

Christ's resurrection assures us that our sins are forgiven and we will be delared 'Not guilty' on the great Judgment Day. Negatively, if, hypothetically, Christ was not raised from the dead, His death does not save – He was only a martyr not the Messiah. *If Christ has not been raised your faith is futile and you are still in your sins* (1 Corinthians 15:17). Says Philip Schaff:-

> 'It was only His resurrection that made His death available for our atonement, justification and salvation; without the resurrection His death would be the grave of our hopes; we should still be unredeemed and under the power

of our sins. A gospel of a dead Saviour would be a contradiction and wretched delusion. This is the reasoning of Paul and its force is irresistable.'

Christ's resurrection then is integral to the Christian's salvation. It is God's vindication of, seal of approval on and satisfaction with the cross-work of Christ. It assures us that our salvation has really been accomplished.

iii. The Pledge of the Saved's Glory

Christ's resurrection is the pledge and promise of better things to come for all those that are His. The full-orbed Christian hope is the resurrection of the body, not some vague, ethereal immortality of the soul. Christ's resurrection is the guarantee of every Christian's resurrection: *Christ has been raised from the dead, the first fruits of those who have fallen asleep* (1 Corinthians 15:20). *If the Spirit of Him who raised Jesus from the dead dwells in you, He who raised Christ Jesus from the dead will give life to your mortal bodies also through His Spirit which dwells in you* (Romans 8:11). *And God raised the Lord and will also raise us up by His power* (1 Corinthians 6:14).

Christian salvation thus awaits its full and final consummation. If we are united by faith to Christ now, we are most certainly saved - and yet not fully so. We are saved in soul but not in body. This full and final salvation of both body and soul will only occur at the return of Christ at the end of the age, when God will create a new heaven and a new earth, and give us bodies perfectly adapted for that perfect environment. *The creation itself will be set free from its bondage to decay and obtain the glorious liberty of the children of God. We know that the whole creation has been groaning in travail together until now, and not only the creation, but we ourselves, who have the first fruits of the Spirit, groan inwardly as we wait for adoption of sons, the redemption of our bodies* (Romans 8:21-23).

The Bible reveals Christ's bodily resurrection as the proto-type of the Christian's resurrection. *We await a Saviour, the Lord Jesus Christ, who will change our lowly body to be like His glorious body, by the power which enables Him even to subject all things to Himself* (Philippians 3:21). What a prospect this is and what a transformation it will be - and what a suitable and agreeable frame to inhabit for all eternity; a redeemed body living on a redeemed earth. It is no wonder that the early Christians anticipated the return of Christ with such eager expectation and longing with the prayer *Marathana! Our Lord come* (1 Corinthians 16:22).

You will no doubt know that life in the present body can be very tough at times. What a comfort then to think of Christ's resurrection. This assures us that life in our present body - with its aches, anxieties, angst, depression, death and decay - is not for ever. *For the trumpet will sound and the dead will be raised imperishable, and we shall be changed. For this perishable nature must put on the imperishable, and this mortal nature must put on immortality. When the perishable puts on the imperishable, and the mortal puts on immortality, then shall come to pass the saying that is written: 'Death is swallowed up in victory.' 'O death where is thy victory? O death where is thy sting?'* (1 Corinthians 15:52-55). Then alone, by God's grace in the crucified, risen Christ, will we enter into *the life which is life indeed* (1 Timothy 6:19).

When Paul preached in Athens *He preached Jesus and the resurrection* (Acts 17:18). May this be our theme and hope as well.

One day the grave could conceal Him no longer
One day the stone rolled away from the door
He had arisen, oe'r death He had conquered
Now is ascended, my Lord evermore

Living, He loved me; dying, He saved me
Buried, He carried my sins far away
Rising He justified freely forever
One day He's coming – O glorious day!

CHAPTER ELEVEN

The Milestone Of His Ascension

So then the Lord Jesus, after He had spoken to them, was taken up
into heaven, and sat down at the right hand of God (Mark 16:19).

And when He had said this, as they were looking on, He was lifted up,
and a cloud took Him out of their sight. And while they were gazing
into heaven as He went, behold, two men stood by them in white
robes, and said, 'Men of Galilee, why do you stand looking into
heaven? This Jesus, who was taken up from you into heaven, will
come in the same way as you saw Him go into heaven' (Acts 1:9-11).

The final milestone in the earthly life of Christ saw Him
ascending miraculously back to His heavenly home on a
cloud, forty days after His resurrection. This culmination
of His earthly ministry is referred to by the Church as 'The Ascension.' Berkhof elaborates:-

> 'The ascension may be described as the visible ascent of
> the Person of the Mediator from earth to heaven, according to His human nature. . . . In a certain sense the ascension may be called the necessary complement and completion of the resurrection. Christ's transition to the higher
> life of glory, begun in the resurrection, was perfected in
> the ascension.'

Theologians sometimes speak of Christ's two states, namely
i. His state of humiliation and ii. His state of exaltation. The

ascension falls into the latter category. The *Shorter Catechism* answers the question 'Wherein consisteth Christ's exaltation?' by stating: 'Christ's exaltation consisteth in His rising again from the dead on the third day, *in ascending up into heaven,* in sitting at the right hand of God the Father, and in coming to judge the world at the last day' (italics mine).

It may be thought that Christ's physical departure would be a cause of much sadness, but this is not in fact the case. Christ has actually gone to heaven prepare a superlative home for us! He said so Himself – *In my Father's house are many rooms; if it were not so, would I have told you that I go to prepare a place for you?* (John 14:2). Also, according to the New Testament, Jesus's departure does not mean His absence. The New Testament takes pains to balance the physical absence of Christ with His spiritual presence in the Person of the Holy Spirit. Jesus said *I will not leave you desolate; I will come to you* (John 14:18) and *it is to your advantage that I go away, for if I do not go away, the Counselor* (the Holy Spirit) *will not come to you; but if I go, I will send Him to you* (John 16:7).

The ascension of the Lord Jesus is generally not given much attention even in Christian circles. Let us therefore redress the balance and consider the meaning of this crowning milestone in the earthly life of the Saviour from four angles:-

1. The Completion of His Mission
2. The Coronation of His Messiahship
3. The Continuation of His Ministry
4. The Coming of His Majesty

1. The Completion of His Mission

Christ's ascension to take His seat at God's right hand proclaims triumphantly 'Mission accomplished'. *When He had made purification for sins, He sat down at the right hand of the Majesty on high* (Hebrews 1:3). *When Christ had offered for all time a single sacrifice for sins, He sat down at the right hand of God* (Hebrews

10:12). How eminently fitting that He Who entered into the world in a supernatural manner, should also exit from the world in a likewise supernatural way. His victorious ascension ties in with His virginal conception – as well as being in line with the rest of His life. Professor Warfield comments:-

> 'It is appropriate that his miraculous life should be set between the great marvels of the virgin birth and the resurrection and ascension. These can appear strange only when the intervening life is looked upon as that of a merely human being . . . From the standpoint of the evangelical writers, and of the entirety of primitive Christianity, which looked upon Jesus not as a merely human being but as God Himself come into the world on a mission of mercy . . . it would be this assumed community with common humanity in mode of entrance into and exit from the earthly life which would seem strange and incredible. The entrance of the Lord of Glory into the world could not but be supernatural. His exit from the world after the work which He had undertaken had been performed, could not fail to bear the stamp of triumph . . .'

Imagine the scene in glory when the Son of God returned home! Psalm 24 seems to give us a prophetic inkling of the celebratory atmosphere: *Lift up your heads, O gates! and be lifted up, O ancient doors! that the King of glory may come in. Who is the King of glory? The Lord of hosts, He is the King of glory* (Psalm 24:9,10).

Golden harps are sounding
Angel voices ring
Pearly gates are opened
Opened for the King
Christ the King of glory
Jesus, King of love
Is gone up in triumph
To His throne above.

2. The Coronation of His Messiahship

The ascension speaks to us of both the enthronement and the reign of King Jesus. Calvin comments:-

> By rising again Christ began to display His glory and good-ness fully, having put behind Him His lowly human life and the shame of the cross. *But it was only by His ascension to heaven that His reign really began.* The apostle bears this out when he says He ascended 'in order to fill the whole universe (Ephesians 4:10) . . .' (*Institutes* II,16,14, italics mine).

Notice that Christ ascended to a particular place and location, namely to 'the right hand of God.' Being seated at the right hand of God, in Scripture, connotes kingly authority, honour, eminence, power, glory and government (see 1 Kings 2:19, Psalms 98:1, 118:15,16, Mark 10:37 et al). Both Peter and Paul give allusions to Christ's kingship by employing this term. Peter wrote of Christ: *who has gone into heaven and is at the right hand of God, with angels, authorities and powers subject to Him* (1 Peter 3:22) and Paul tells of Christ's being seated *at His right hand in the heavenly places, far above all rule, authority and power and dominion, and above every name that is named, not only in this age but also in that which is to come; and He has put all things under His feet and has made Him the head over all things for the Church* (Ephesians 1:20-22).

Christ's ascension therefore reminds us that He is King. Jesus admitted as much to Pilate upon close questioning: *You say that I am a king. For this I was born, and for this I have come into the world* . . . (John 18:37). Jesus's kingship is one facet of His being the Messiah. As Messiah He unites the threefold office of prophet, priest and king in His one Person. Jesus is the Messiah – great David's Greater Son – and His reign is universal, *for He must reign until He has put all His enemies under His feet* (1 Corinthians

15:25). The *Shorter Catechism* defines Christ's kingship most helpfully when it states 'Christ executeth the office of a king in subduing us to Himself, in ruling and defending us, and in restraining and conquering all His and our enemies' (Q. 25). Berkhof amplifies concerning this ascended reign of Christ at God's right hand by pointing out that here:-

'The Mediator received the reigns of government over the Church and over the universe, and is made to share in the corresponding glory. This does not mean that Christ was not King of Zion up to this time, but that now He is publically inaugurated as God-man, and as such receives the government of the Church and of heaven and earth, and enters solemnly upon the actual administration of the power committed to Him . . .

'The Bible most frequently connects the session with the kingly rule of Christ . . . He rules and protects His Church by His Spirit, and also governs it through His appointed officers. He has all the forces of heaven under His command: the angels are His messengers, always ready to convey His blessings to the saints, and to guard them against surrounding dangers. He exercises authority over the forces of nature, and over all the powers that are hostile to the Kingdom of God; and will so continue to reign until He has subjected the last enemy.'

The head that once was crowned with thorns
Is crowned with glory now
A royal diadem adorns
The mighty Victor's brow

The highest place that heaven affords
Is His by sovereign right
The King of kings, and Lord of lords
And heaven's eternal Light.

3. The Continuation of His Ministry

Although Christ's ascension brought a spectacular conclusion and consummation to His earthly mission, paradoxically, it also reminds us that His saving ministry still continues, chiefly in the application of the salvation He accomplished on earth to the souls of His elect people. Salvation is applied to God's people by Christ's Spirit, and Christ's continual intercession in heaven ensures that His people are kept securely in the good of the salvation He accomplished on earth. We shall shortly consider something of Christ's present high priestly ministry, a ministry which He undertakes for His own at God's right hand. Whilst Christ is seated at God's right hand, He is certainly not inactive. His ministry continues – and it will continue until all the elect are safely gathered in. The *Westminster Confession* states:

> 'To all those for whom Christ hath purchased redemption, He doth certainly and effectually apply and communicate the same; making intercession for them, and revealing unto them, in and by the Word, the mysteries of salvation; effectually persuading them by His Spirit to believe and obey, and governing their hearts by His Word and Spirit . . .' (VIII,viii).

i. The Holy Spirit of Christ

The Shorter Catechism reminds us 'We are made partakers of the redemption purchased by Christ by the effectual application of it to us by His Holy Spirit' (Q. 29). Ten days after His ascension - on the day we now know as the day of Pentecost - Christ poured out His Holy Spirit on the earth as He promised. Scripture links the ascension and Pentecost in a most definite way. John makes an editorial comment on Jesus's earthly ministry thus: *as yet the Spirit had not been given, because Jesus was not yet glorified* (John 7:39), and on the actual day of the Pentecostal outpouring, Peter explained to the gathered crowd: *Being therefore at the right hand of God, and having received from the Father the promise of the Holy Spirit, He has poured out this which you see and hear* (Acts 2:33).

ii. The Heavenly Supplication of Christ

The fact that Christ intercedes for His own is a source of immeasurable comfort to His people. Paul rejoiced in *Christ Jesus . . . who is at the right hand of God, who indeed intercedes for us* (Romans 8:34). The writer to the Hebrews wrote in similar encouraging tones: *Since then we have a great high priest who has passed through the heavens, Jesus, the Son of God, let us hold fast our confession* (Hebrews 4:14) and assures us in Hebrews 9:24 that *Christ has entered into heaven itself, now to appear in the presence of God on our behalf.* Berkhof expands:-

> 'The Bible . . . connects the priestly work with Christ's session at the right hand of God. . . Christ is continually presenting His completed sacrifice to the Father as the sufficient basis for the bestowal of the pardoning grace of God. He is constantly applying His sacrificial work, and making it effective in the justification and sanctification of sinners. Moreover, He is ever making intercession for those that are His, pleading for their acceptance on the basis of His completed sacrifice, and for their safe-keeping in the world, and making their prayers and services acceptable to God . . .'

Hallelujah! *He is able for all time to save those who draw near to God through Him, since He always lives to make intercession for them* (Hebrews 7:25).

> *Before the throne of God above*
> *I have a strong, a perfect plea*
> *A great High Priest, whose name is Love*
> *Who ever lives and pleads for me.*

Finally, notice that the milestone of Christ's ascension also tells us of:-

4. The Coming of His Majesty

In Luke's account of the ascension we read:- *And while they were gazing into heaven as He went, behold two men stood by them in white robes, and said 'Men of Galilee, why do you stand looking into heaven? This Jesus, who was taken from you into heaven, will come in the same way as you saw Him go into heaven'* (Acts 1:10,11).

The ascension then reminds us that Jesus is coming again. Jesus is going to return to reign in the same manner as He ascended to heaven – personally, visibly, gloriously (clouds in Scripture often connote God's glory) and, we should emphasise, literally. John records the Event with prophetic foresight in the opening of the last book of the inspired volume: *Behold, He is coming with the clouds, and every eye shall see Him* (Revelation 1:7). This return of Christ is the goal of all history, and is referred to aptly by Paul as *our blessed hope, the appearing of the glory of our great God and Saviour Jesus Christ* (Titus 2:13). When Christ returns - which He most surely will - time will end and eternity will begin.

At the Second Coming of Christ, His majesty now latent will be patent. His government now spiritual will be universal. Jesus shall reign! *For He must reign until He has put all His enemies under His feet* (1 Corinthians 15:25). If the glorious ascension of Christ tells us nothing else, it proclaims in actions that speak louder than words that *God has highly exalted Him and bestowed on Him the name which is above every name, that at the name of Jesus every knee should bow, in heaven and on earth and under the earth, and every tongue confess that Jesus Christ is Lord to the glory of God the Father* (Philippians 2:9-11).

Immortal honours rest on Jesus' head
My God, my portion and my living bread
In Him I live, upon Him cast my care
He saves from death, destruction and despair

O that my soul could love and praise Him more
His beauties trace His majesty adore
Live near His heart, upon His bosom lean
Obey His voice, and all His will esteem.

SOLI DEO GLORIA